Do you often find yourself doing things for others that you don't want to do?

When someone talks about their parents, do you immediately feel guilty because you haven't phoned yours lately?

Your boss screams, "The Good Lord must love stupid people, he sure made a bunch of them!" Do you know for a fact that he means you?

YOU DON'T HAVE TO BE A VICTIM ANYMORE.

Expert manipulators know how to make you feel bad—and get what they want by doing it. By learning to spot the hidden messages of guilt and fear, you can decode the messages of manipulation—and reclaim control of your decisions and your life.

STOP BEING MANIPULATED

STOP BEING MANIPULATED

How to Neutralize the Bullies, Bosses, and Brutes in Your Life

GEORGE H. GREEN, Ph.D., and CAROLYN COTTER, MBA

BERKLEY BOOKS, NEW YORK

STOP BEING MANIPULATED

A Berkley Book / published by arrangement with
the authors

PRINTING HISTORY
Berkley edition / April 1995

The Penguin Putnam Inc. World Wide Web site address is
http://www.penguinputnam.com

ISBN: 0-425-14686-3

BERKLEY®
Berkley Books are published by The Berkley Publishing Group,
a member of Penguin Putnam Inc.,
375 Hudson Street, New York, New York 10014.
BERKLEY and the "B" design
are trademarks belonging to Berkley Publishing Corporation.

PRINTED IN THE UNITED STATES OF AMERICA

15 14 13 12 11 10 9 8 7 6

ACKNOWLEDGMENTS

Special acknowledgment goes to the numerous clients and students of Dr. Green who helped him formulate these techniques.

The authors want to thank our spouses, Miriam Green and Dick Cotter, for their patience and counsel. Without their assistance, and the help and cooperation of our children, Becki and Lewis Green, and Kate and David Cotter, this project could never have been completed.

Dr. Green would like to acknowledge his brother, Dr. Stephen L. Green, who was encouraging by being impressed!

Our gratitude goes to Elizabeth Lyon of Lyon's Literary Service, Eugene, Oregon, for being instrumental in the creation, nurturing, and completion of this project.

Our respect and admiration extend to our champion and literary agent, Denise Marcil, who believed in us.

Our appreciation goes to Elizabeth Beier, senior editor at The Berkley Publishing Group, and the rest of the staff who gave so generously of their time and talents.

And to our family, friends, and community who advised and supported us, and provided inspiration along with perspiration, to keep this book moving along, especially: Emily Hughes and Lyndon Duke for their sage advice; the Warrens, Helen Reed, and Frs. Ralph and Jonathan for their hand-holding expertise; author Kristen Ingram for her wit; and, in loving memory, to Dorothy, whose life was a sparkle.

Finally, Dr. Green acknowledges the efforts of his coauthor, Carolyn, who saw the vision and kept it alive.

CONTENTS

CHAPTER 1

Neutralizing Manipulation

Your family is on their way home from camping. You've timed your travel through a popular coastal town so that you arrive at 4:00 P.M., at the beginning of The Tenth Annual Fish Fry, a Chamber of Commerce fund-raiser, featuring all the fresh fish that you can eat. By being first in line, you can eat an early dinner and be on your way before dark. Or so you thought. You've been in line for over half an hour: it's now 4:45 P.M. The fish have been frying forever and the corn has boiled past pulp. The salad and beans are tired, and volunteers are milling around. About one hundred people are in line behind you.

You go up to a nicely dressed woman who is spooning tartar sauce into what appears to be her two hundredth tiny paper cup and ask politely, "Do you know how much longer it will be?" She replies, "The bread hasn't arrived yet." Trying to be helpful, you suggest that maybe they could go ahead and serve everything but the bread, so out-of-towners could be on their way. She blasts you with, "And *who* died and put you in charge of this show?" You ask nicely, "Well, who is the person in charge here?"

She responds with, "*Everyone's* in charge here—just a whole bunch of chiefs."

At this point, you are sorely tempted to do something clever and unique with the tartar sauce, or at least to have the last word. But instead you choose to neutralize the remarks to avoid a confrontation. By neutralizing this encounter at the time it occurs, you will be left with a minimum of crummy feelings.

And how to avoid feeling crummy in manipulative situations is what this book is all about. Neutralizing manipulation. Throughout the book we will use the word "manipulation" to mean: an encounter in which someone else attempts to control *how* you feel, or *how* you behave, or *how* you think, without your permission, and it causes you discomfort as a result. Rude, insulting, and insensitive comments directed toward you also make you feel crummy, and they, too, are included in our definition of manipulation. We are not talking about teaching your children good manners by rewarding them appropriately. This is not a book about positive reinforcement for positive behavior, inspiration, patterning, teaching, and loving guidance. This book hopefully will not be a struggle in semantics. We will deal only with neutralizing the negative aspects of manipulation. Let's simplify our definition of manipulation: if an encounter leaves you feeling crummy, it probably involves manipulation of some sort. We'll use our Quick Rule: "If it looks like a goat, acts like a goat, and sounds like a goat, it probably is a goat."

Why do people try to manipulate you? Believe it or not, people do this so they can feel better about themselves. Herein lies an irony: the person who is trying to manipulate you views *you* as having greater strength or power than he or she does.

If we stop and think about this for a moment, we can ask ourselves how many people, unless they are truly malicious or very sick, attempt to manipulate a powerless person. They simply don't spend their energy doing that. *The manipulators attempt to control someone whom they admire, like, or are afraid of; or whom they perceive has more control over his or her own life than the manipulators have over theirs.*

In most successful manipulations, a direct relationship exists between the severity of the manipulation and the degree to which the target of the manipulation feels guilty, fearful, ashamed, or humiliated. We will use the descriptive word "slimed" to convey the negative feelings in these instances. You can almost see the transference of energy. The manipulator pulls a real coup and leaves the victim speechless. The manipulator becomes almost giddy with power and energy, while the victim becomes depressed and uncomfortable. This reaction, one laughing, one almost in tears, gives a Dracula-type reality to the manipulation. The manipulator seems to feed off the energy of the victim of the manipulation. The next time you observe, or are the unwilling participant in a manipulation, notice the body language and the personality changes in everyone involved. The manipulator becomes the aggressor, and the manipulated becomes apologetic. Despite the words that may be spoken by the parties involved, the energy is one of creating control where none existed or was needed except in the mind of the manipulator. For example:

SPOKEN MESSAGE, PLEASANT VOICE: "You know I'd *really* appreciate it if all of this work could be done before you go home." UNSPOKEN MESSAGE: "*I'm* the boss, and you'd better do it or else!" DEEPER MESSAGE: "You're always so efficient that I feel lazy compared to you!"

You probably won't be able to witness these encounters in quite the same way again. Yet, it's helpful to remember that the manipulator acts out of fear and insecurity, thriving on other people's power. So, in reality, *the manipulators are actually paying you a very high compliment.* At the least they perceive that *you have more power* than they have and they want some of it. At most, *they are envious,* they admire you, they like you, and thus feel compelled to try to control you. If they just came up to you and said, "Hey, I really admire you, and I'd like to control you so I can feel better. . . . Let's do lunch!" you'd check in with your nearest reality connection. But it doesn't work that way. Manipulators *need* to control you and will generally use one or two weapons to achieve that end.

What are the not-so-subtle weapons of the garden-variety manipulator? Guilt and fear! You don't need an advanced degree in psychology to define and distinguish between the two. Nor to recognize the discomfort caused by each. However, the *successful use* of guilt and fear as weapons of the manipulator is dependent, to some degree, on how each of us *reacts* to those weapons. We will explore guilt and fear further in the next two chapters.

After that, we will introduce the five levels to stop manipulation. The techniques are simple, but they do require a bit of thought, practice, and discussion. If you do that small amount of work, the techniques will become incorporated into your very being, and will become automatic. You will recognize every manipulative attempt for what it is and be able to neutralize it automatically.

The word "manipulation" is derived from the Latin word *manus,* meaning "hand." When people try to manipulate you, they try to "handle" you, don't they? Therefore, you need a self-defensive, noncombative, but powerful system to avoid being handled against your wishes. The martial arts meet this requirement. The five-level system presented in this book draws from the philosophy and principles of the soft (unarmed) martial arts.

If we were to summarize the basic concept of the martial arts, it is to protect yourself while doing minimal damage to your opponent. This can be a hard concept for a person with a win-lose mentality. This is a hard concept in the shark-infested waters of today. This is a hard concept for most people in our Western culture. We will suggest a strategy, however, to neutralize manipulation and avoid counterattack.

In the West, not much was known until fairly recently about the martial arts techniques because this knowledge was imparted through training and was not written down. A large part of its value lay in secrecy.

The martial arts began their development several thousand years ago in the Far East. The basic reason for their existence was the necessity for self-defense in a place that didn't allow the common man or peasant to have standard weapons. Several schools of martial arts appeared. Some used common farm implements and turned them into lethal weapons through practice. Others stressed using hands and feet as weapons. Some combined both.

There are basically two types of martial arts: the hard martial arts and the soft martial arts. Some of the hard arts use weapons (self-devised, as with the Philippine stick fighters), and others rely on the hands and feet as weapons (like karate). The soft martial arts primarily use evasive tactics and joint locks and holds to immobilize the attacker. The soft martial arts also rely heavily on using the force of the attacker to defeat the attacker.

The five levels presented in this book utilize the soft (unarmed) martial arts: "A martial art that has two main principles: first, the mind dictates the action; second, the opponent's own force is used to defeat him or her.'' (Howard Reid and Michael Croucher, *The Fighting Arts*. New York: Simon & Schuster, 1983, p. 229.)

Yielding, flow, mental control: all can be used to your advantage when countering a verbal attack. When you come under attack by a manipulator, you need to view the attack as a martial arts expert would. You don't want to fall apart and get all emotional. If you lie coldcocked on the floor, you aren't any help to yourself or anyone else. The name of the game is to get your emotions out of the way and let your mind automatically and instantaneously take charge—let your mind use the five-level system that you'll learn here.

The soft martial artist deals in *real time*, that is, "the now." Worrying about the future and regretting our past prevents us from being alert, receptive, and relaxed. Neutralization cannot occur when we get in our own way.

The soft martial artist is always receptive. This includes being open, aware, and relaxed. It is only by being relaxed that we are able to receive, then deflect, then defuse, then neutralize. (Father Bryce McProud, Episcopal priest and soft martial artist, St. Matthew's Episcopal Church, Eugene, Oregon.)

When you suspect you are the target of a manipulation, just ask yourself, "Who is in control? Who has the greater power? The bully beating everyone up? Or the person whose power rests on giving freedom of choice to another?"

An important thing to remember, but hard for any of us to do, is to realize that manipulation, like *attack* in the martial arts, is *not personal*. It is personal only in the sense that your opponent considers you important enough or strong enough to attack in the first place.

The martial arts skills stayed mostly in the Far East until this century. Now self-defense classes are taught everywhere. Some are pure, teaching the principles that accompany a specific art, that is, karate, judo, jujitsu, aikido, kung fu, etc.

Others teach you to defend yourself, period. Watch some classes where women are taught to defend themselves (they look like fighting bobcats). Women are literally taught to go for the assailant's eyes, ears, and groin. Using the tiger's claw, they learn to rip the muscles; using white snake eyes, they punch at the eyes; a groin kick does the rest. We, the authors, feel that these aggressive techniques are more like lessons on how to counterattack than on how to neutralize. They may work well in a life-or-death situation, but verbal attack is not usually so extreme. (However, a few examples do come to mind.)

The soft (unarmed) martial arts therefore serve as the basis for the five-level system presented here: ju-jitsu, aikido, and t'ai chi ch'uan.

> The difference between power that runs in a straight line and that which curves in toward the opponent, is the difference between the hard and soft versions of the martial arts. The straight away power has an end: it terminates when impact is made. In T'ai Chi Ch'uan, which uses circular force, the movement is never done, it moves right through the opponent and as it moves gathers strength for the next action. . . . The player becomes selfless and utilizes the opponent's strength. . . . The opponent's strength is neutralized, putting him at a disadvantage. Extreme softness always prevails over extreme hardness.'' (William Logan and Herman Petras, *Handbook of the*

Martial Arts and Self-Defense. New York: Funk &
Wagnalls, 1975.)

The soft martial arts are a philosophy as well as a set of
self-defense techniques. You actually change the rules. You
are not limited to your past bag of tricks. The rules are
changed when someone is up against a different force in
fighting, aren't they? If everyone knows the rules, the elements of surprise and suspense are missing.

You *can* defend yourself. You can use the manipulators'
own force to neutralize them in your life. As you work with
these self-defense techniques, they will become second-
nature and will kick in automatically.

That day will come when you can spot a manipulation a
mile away, recognize it as a compliment, and automatically
implement the appropriate level to neutralize it and walk
away unharmed. Then you can say, "Today, I earned my
verbal black belt!"

THE MANY FACES OF MANIPULATION

Manipulation is almost everywhere, and it comes in all
sizes and shapes. It shows no mercy concerning age, sex,
or race. While manipulation is executed largely on the *subconscious* level, the manipulator is, quite simply, trying to
get some of the strength and power of another person who
is viewed as having greater strength to start with. The person being targeted ends up feeling slimed and falling prey
to guilt, anger, or fear.

Perhaps at this point you're wondering if it's possible
that you have no manipulation in your life. This may be
possible, but you might want to try taking the following
little quiz.

How Manipulated Are You?

1. Do you find yourself often doing things for others that you don't want to do?
2. Do you find yourself buying things that you later find you don't really need or even want?
3. When someone talks about their parents, do you immediately feel guilty because you haven't phoned yours the past month, week, day, or hour?
4. Does someone in your environment act like you are crazy?
5. Do you find yourself buying unnecessarily expensive shoes, clothes, computers, and sports cars for your teenager?
6. Do you feel guilty because you don't go regularly to a place of worship? Does going to your place of worship leave you feeling even worse than before?
7. Your boss screams, "The Good Lord must love stupid people, he sure made a bunch of them!" Do you know for a fact that he means you?
8. When you receive a telephone call from the principal of your son's school, do you feel like disavowing all knowledge and telling her that she has the wrong Mrs. _____?
9. Do you feel compelled to hang Aunt Martha's painting (the one of the cross-eyed camel) over your living room sofa even though Aunt Martha's been dead for six years now?
10. Did you just discover that PMS is a medical condition, not short for "persistent mean sarcasm"?

If you answered yes to any of the above, manipulation has seeped into your life. You're not alone. Virtually everyone has known the frustration, and oftentimes the embarrassment, that manipulation brings—from feeling somewhat uncomfortable to downright speechless. Let's face it: we all eventually manipulate someone else at one time or another, although it is usually done unintentionally. Sometimes we even try to manipulate ourselves into doing or not doing certain things, through the use of guilt and fear.

Manipulation can be of a personal nature or an impersonal nature. It can be blatantly aggressive or amazingly passive. For instance, how would you judge the following situation? The young man brings flowers to the young lady. Is this manipulation? Is he bringing them to her out of love and consideration? If so, then your answer "no," is correct. No manipulation there. Or is he saying, "Like me, like me"? If she likes him, there is no discomfort, and hence no manipulation as we define it. But what if the lady can't stand to see him coming and his attentions are bothering her? In that case, your answer "yes" is correct. If he goes on to become a stalker, then this manipulation has turned into abuse. It has crossed over the line into unacceptable behavior. In fact, laws are being passed that outlaw that offensive behavior.

What about the man who says to the woman, "I love you. . . . If you really love me, show it and come to bed with me." If it's manipulation, he may use both guilt and fear. Guilt that she doesn't love him as much as she should. Fear that he'll leave her for another who does. But what if she responds this way? "I thought you'd never ask." Then this is not really manipulation, is it?

How about the personal and aggressive nature of lawsuits? Passing the buck. Shifting the blame. The blame must go somewhere, and the person holding it decides he or she simply doesn't want it anymore and tries to pass it on. On the one hand, if a wrong has been committed, and someone or something else has caused it, an attempt to make right what went wrong and be compensated is reasonable. On the other hand, if an attempt is made to shift the blame elsewhere when there is at least shared responsibility, manipulation enters the picture. And where this line is drawn can be difficult in a market economy that says "buyer beware" in one breath and "protect the consumer" in the next.

How about the impersonal, but no less powerful, realm of politicians, preachers, coaches, and others who have potential power over others? Here the appeal to the nobler or the higher self can be either manipulative or inspirational. Watch a coach pepping up a team beforehand, "I'm counting on you, you can do it, you've got the guts, the will, the training . . ." You can see that the encouragement to get that team to go the extra mile, that says, "I know you can do it," reflects a glory shared between the person doing the encouraging and the person expending the effort. Both win. However, taken to the extreme, even this can border on the abusive. Forcing someone beyond his or her limits can lead to physical injury and mental/emotional strain. The coach that makes his team play rough in order to win at any cost becomes debasing rather than uplifting. The politician can act like a noble statesman, inspiring his county, state, or country to its highest potential. Or the politician can serve her own selfish interests and become another Machiavelli.

How do you handle the constant bombardment of advertising and persistent salespeople? If you want and can afford the product and suffer no buyer's remorse, it's not manipulation. If, however, you succumb to buying expensive items you can't afford or feel inadequate in some way because you can't have a particular thing, then you've been manipulated. Advertising can use heavy doses of guilt and fear, delivered with the promise of money, power, status, or love, in order to accomplish its purpose—namely getting you to buy a certain product or service.

Advertising creates a need or a want whether one truly exists or not. A need to look, smell, and be your best by buying the clothes, deodorants, and eyeglasses that the beautiful models have. A need to protect yourself and your family (e.g., with smoke alarms and state-of-the-art new cars). Fears and guilts are exploited. Will your co-workers, friends, and neighbors think less of you for driving that older model car? Are you irresponsible for not going into debt to get all the newest safety features? What kind of a parent are you for not purchasing the latest educational tools for your children, to assist them in learning? What does it say about your love for your wife when you don't even give her a tenth anniversary diamond ring?

Lest you think that all manipulators are overtly aggressive, consider these three examples of passive manipulation. It is amazing how creative we human beings are in the manner in which we express manipulation. For instance, take the person who says that he or she will do X or Y or Z. And doesn't. Like raising procrastination to an art form. Pure immobility. "I'll get the garage cleaned out tomorrow for you, for sure." This then gets played 365 days a year until someone else does it or everyone involved moves.

Some people use the "I'm-little-I'm-weak" variety of manipulation on others. This form is personified by the grandmother in the *Anne of Green Gables* series. Don't open the shutters; the light will blind me. Don't upset me; I'll have a heart attack and die. Everyone within a mile tries to avoid doing anything to shake her up. Everyone within a mile ends up doing exactly what the grandmother, in this example, wants.

In the third example, the manipulator takes the blame

and exaggerates it. Here's where blame is not passed around for fear of hanging onto it. Quite the opposite. Here the manipulator plays out a warped version of virtual reality: "You can't fire me, I quit." Or, "I'm a lousy driver, I proved it; I wrecked the car." You can't blame me, I'll take all the blame, real or not, thank you very much. You can't manipulate me through fear or guilt. I'll get there first. Now *you* have to make me feel better. This is a twist on honestlies or honest lies as we refer to them in Level Five.

To further explore the faces of manipulation, let's review the following *ABC's of the Manipulator*. Please keep in mind the issues of power and control, and the manipulator's weapons: guilt and fear.

The ABC'S of the Manipulator

A = Use ANGER whenever possible. This puts the other person squarely on the defensive and forces him or her to counterattack using your rules. For example, "Where the &^ %$# have you been? It's after midnight!"

B = BELITTLE another person. Especially in public. "How *could* you have locked your keys in the car for the second time this week? Even my dog is smarter than that!"

C = CONTROL, CONTROL, CONTROL. The more people the merrier. The more people you can control, the better you feel.

D = DENY manipulating. "Who me?" "Do what?"

E = EXAGGERATE your own importance so that everyone knows what a truly powerful person you are. For example, "I've got to run, see you later. No time to visit now. I'm expecting a phone call. A *really* important one—Washington, you know."

F = Use FEAR whenever possible. It's guaranteed to be a major weapon in your arsenal. For example, "Hey, I know you're flying out tomorrow on vacation, but I'd be really careful if I were you. Heard there were a string of robberies in your neighborhood . . . and that the last three flights had to land on foam at the airport . . . no big deal . . . but if I were you . . ."

G = Use GUILT the rest of the time. Combined with fear, use of guilt guarantees you'll go far as a manipulator. For example, "That's okay. Go spend the weekend with your friends. It doesn't matter. I'm only your mother. I want you to have a really nice time. Honest. I mean, the fact that it's my birthday next month . . . Go on, I'll be fine, honest."

H = Use HONESTLIES whenever possible. "I know I shouldn't tell you this, but it's for your own good. You really need to know what I just heard your sister say about you."

I = INTIMIDATE another person, especially using rude remarks and body language. For example, "Is that *all* you've managed to get done? . . . Jeepers, you'll be lucky to get that finished by the end of the year."

J = JUDGE others without mercy. For example, "He is the stupidest person I've ever known."

K = KNOW it all! For example, "California, of course. Where else would Berkley Publishers be located? Huh? Huh?"

L = LIVE other people's lives for them. You know better than they do what they need. For example, "I sure wouldn't wear that tie with those trousers.

I mean nobody would wear that color tie with those color trousers.''

M = MANIPULATE, MANIPULATE, MANIPULATE.

N = Use NASTY comments over kind ones. It'll start another person's day off with a bang. For example, ''You look like &^%$^. Are you sick or what?''

O = ORGANIZE the heck out of everyone else. For example, You: ''Why do you keep the salt and pepper shakers on the left side of this cabinet? It would be a lot more labor efficient to put them over here.'' Them: ''Because that's where I've put them for the past twenty-five years, before you retired.''

P = POWER, POWER, POWER. Get it anywhere you can. ''I sure nailed the paperboy one good, I did. I called the circulation manager. I told him I want my newspaper by 6:30 A.M., not thirty seconds late. Every time it's thirty seconds late or more, I'll call. And see if he gets a tip this month. Ha!''

Q = QUIT any discussion and march off in a huff if you don't get your way immediately. For example, ''Well, if that's the way you see things, I won't be a party to this. It just won't work. I'm leaving.''

R = ''MAKE RUDE'' whenever possible. Rude and crude are in. Forget polite comments and gentleness of manner unless it positions you for the kill later. ''**&^%$*()*&.!''

S = Use SHOULDLIES wherever possible. ''You really should lose weight you know, Harold, it'd make you feel better.'' And watch the transference of power between Harold and you.

T = Verbally THREATEN another whenever possible. ''Heard a rumor that the bosses are thinking of consolidating various departments. Have you polished up your résumé, yet?''

U = USE others to achieve your own ends. Think like Machiavelli. What would he do in this situation? Be ruthless.

V = Target another's VULNERABILITY and go for it. If given the choice between hitting on the woman in the office who is married to the Marine or hitting on the single mom with four children . . . You got it.

W = WIN at any cost. Never say you're sorry or that you've made a mistake. This helps ensure your power base.

X = X-PECT others to do what you want. After all, that's why they were placed on this planet, right?

Y = YELL at others a lot. It puts them on the defensive and establishes once and for all just who is the boss.

Z = ZERO in on another person's guilt and fear like a heat-seeking missile. Then use these to your advantage.

The many faces of manipulation can be viewed as a sliding scale. One end is considered no manipulation and a function of occupying the planet with other people and wanting to do or have certain things through your own work and/or cooperation with others. In its purest form, this low end of the scale is love and concern for another, where you stand to gain nothing—no power, no control—simple interactions with another person. The opposite extreme is abuse in its various forms. In abuse situations, it is vital to contact and seek help from a trusted minister or rabbi, from local community resources, or from professional counselors.

Most of the manipulation we'll be addressing in this book refers to garden-variety manipulation (somewhere in the middle of the sliding scale), at home, at work, and in social settings. Guilt and fear are the major weapons of the manipulator. Our individual reactions to the manipulator and the manipulation vary but usually involve guilt and fear (imposed or self-imposed). But please keep in mind that what one person might label as manipulative aggravating behavior might not bother a different person in the same way.

Take the case of Mary and John. Mary works for the city and has to be at work by 8:00 A.M., earlier if she wants to get a parking space. John works for a roofing company as a roofer. John has blood sugar problems, and it is important that he take his lunch to work each day, since he is seldom near a fast-food place or a restaurant when he is on the job. To skip lunch is simply not medically smart for him. The responsibility for making his sandwiches falls on Mary since John can never get it together in the early morning to make them himself. Mary has tried freezing those sandwiches the night before, but they really come out a soggy mass. She resents making the sandwiches and has attempted to structure early mornings so John can be encouraged to take on this responsibility himself. But to no avail. John never gets mad at Mary for not making his sandwiches. He merely shrugs his shoulders and makes a comment like "Won't hurt me to miss a lunch now and then. . . . I need to lose a pound or two anyway."

Mary makes those sandwiches out of guilt and fear. She feels guilty that she resents making the sandwiches. After all, she's his wife, isn't she? And it's not that big a deal. And she feels fear. What if John's blood sugar should fall so low that he topples off the roof and breaks both legs? Then she'd really feel guilty, plus she'd inherit the additional responsibility of having to haul him around everywhere, since he wouldn't be able to drive himself until the casts were removed. Not to mention the rehab and physical therapy. Can you see how guilt, fear, and worry are what's really bothering her? Not the five minutes in the morning that it takes to make the sandwiches.

And maybe, just maybe, another wife somewhere has no guilt, no fear, no worry in the exact same situation. She simply regards making those sandwiches as routine, like brushing her teeth in the morning. Not even a second thought.

And maybe, just maybe, another wife somewhere lets her husband be in charge of fixing his lunch or not, taking it or not, and figures if he gets low blood sugar, he'll get down off the roof before he falls off it.

We all come equipped with our own guilt and fear and often make the mistake of projecting them onto other people. Guilt can be imposed upon us by others, or we can self-impose it. Likewise, our fears may trap us into feeling and acting a certain way, when in fact, no external threat exists in the situation. The threat is internal and often blown out of proportion.

Whether it is external or internal, we are still talking manipulation—by others or by ourselves. If you can learn about everyday manipulation, the kind addressed here, which falls somewhere in the middle of the scale, you can recognize it, neutralize it, and avoid it in the future. If you can indeed recognize a situation in which you are being manipulated, either at the hands of others or at your own hands, you are on the first step to wholeness.

You do not have to be a victim anymore.

CHAPTER 2

Guilt

One of the Two Major Weapons of the Manipulator

As we explore the five levels of countering manipulation, we will pursue some analogies to the soft (unarmed) martial arts self-defense techniques and principles. The martial arts have taught us that we do not need to destroy our attacker (the manipulator) to win the battle.

Before we launch into these techniques, it is important to understand the first of the two major weapons of the manipulator: GUILT. In order to deal defensively with the manipulator, we need to identify the major weapons used.

Let's take the true case of Walt, an accountant. Walt is a member of a support group. It is one of the many useful support groups that exist to help us cope with life's difficulties and tragedies. Also a member of this group is Lucille, who appears to be in her mid-nineties. Lucille zeroes in on Walt at every meeting. She obviously loves his attention. One evening, before the weekly meeting, she corners Walt, and in front of a small group of people says, "Hey, Walt, I brought all my medical bills and insurance stuff for the past six months. I have three insurances and everything's all messed up. Would you straighten it out?"

Walt looks at a carton full of old bills, collection notices, balances due, and insurance forms. It looks like an accoun-

19

tant's nightmare. Besides, Walt knows nothing about medical billing, insurance, and Medicare. And finally, Walt is so busy at work that he's lucky to make it to the support group, period.

Can you feel what Walt is going through? He feels sorry for her. She obviously needs help. He feels peer pressure: *What will the others think of me if I say no to Lucille?* Who could refuse a senior citizen in distress? In short, Walt knows that he will feel guilty saying no.

So Walt says, "Okay, I'll take them home and work on them." Now Walt feels crummy. Walt feels manipulated. Walt even feels angry, tricked, and trapped.

Can you see where his sense of ethics generates a self-imposed guilt on Walt? Maybe Walt's grandmother or mother needed help at one time.

Walt is being manipulated. Does Lucille see Walt as having more power (and ability) than she has? Yes. Is Lucille paying Walt a compliment? Yes. Is Lucille deliberately trying to hurt Walt? No. Does she sense the vulnerability he may feel because of his guilt about his own grandmother? Yes.

What is "guilt"? The feeling of responsibility. We are guilty when we have done something wrong. We have made a mistake. And who is the first person to let us know that we have made a mistake? Not us. It all begins with parental disapproval. We are caught as a child doing something wrong, and we are punished. And now, five years later or fifty years later, we are still seeking parental approval. It doesn't change anything that our parents may actually approve of us now. They may even be dead. We are still seeking approval from the time when we were a child. How do we get approval from a memory? How do we get approval from a ghost?

Guilt feels crummy, like being slimed, and we are stuck

with it until we permit ourselves a figurative shower, emotional cleansing. Guilt, itself, is neutral. It is the secondary feeling (feeling guilty) that causes our discomfort: anger, irritability, depression, feelings of oppression and the desire to get even.

We can all identify with the light bulb jokes: How many _____(you fill in the blank) does it take to change a light bulb? Ten. One to hold the light bulb and the other nine to turn the ladder. How many psychotherapists does it take to change a light bulb? None. The light bulb has to be willing to change. And finally, how many children does it take to change a light bulb for an overprotective, controlling mother? "None, thank you, I can sit in the dark. It won't kill me."

In order for guilt to work, we have to agree to that guilt. We have to agree to take on that *implied responsibility*. We have to feel we need to do something which we are not doing, or stop doing something that we are doing.

Let's take an example. Suppose that you are late meeting your friend for lunch. Your friend is waiting for you. When you get there, you feel guilty. Why do you feel guilty? There may be two reasons: you have self-imposed the guilt, and/or the other person is imposing it on you. How does the other person impose it? He or she may glance at a watch and say, "I don't know if we even have enough time now for lunch. I thought you were never going to get here." Then what do you do? You start making excuses. "Traffic was awful." "I overslept." "My pet orangutan has PMS, and I had to sit with her." No matter what you say, it does not seem to get rid of the bad feelings. The feelings are stuck there, as if someone slimed you. It's an unclean feeling.

But what if the other person is not imposing guilt on you? You show up, and he or she says, "Great, you're here, let's go to lunch.'' Your friend doesn't say or do anything negative. But you still feel just awful. This is self-imposed guilt. You have done that to yourself; you have created responsibility the other person has not even given you. Why are you doing that? Who told you that you should always be on time? Your parents, perhaps?

Most of our parents, unless they were flat-out malicious, did the very best they could to raise us. They fully thought they were doing their best. They may have been completely incompetent, but it came from their best shot. They did the best they could. We are *not* bashing parents.

THE IRONY: FEELING GUILTY ABOUT LETTING GO OF GUILT

One feels guilty about letting go of guilt, because conceptualizing what it is like on the other side of that wall—freedom from guilt—is hard.

Those people who feel guilty about letting go of guilt usually feel that if they give up guilt, they are letting someone (whom?) down. That means, by not feeling guilty, they are hurting someone. By feeling guilty, they are hurting only themselves; and if they hurt themselves, then it's all right. If they hurt someone else, then it isn't all right. Does that sound like a martyr? Does that sound like someone who would like to sit alone in the dark? The overprotective mother said, ''It's okay, it won't kill me!'' Most likely such an individual would be thinking, *I don't feel good about myself, and if I did, I'm not sure I'd deserve to. Besides, if I lose control of the people around me, no one will care about me. I must remind everyone of my importance so they don't forget me.* At some level she is probably aware that her expectations that people won't care are unrealistic, but the drive to satisfy insecurity is so strong that she is unable to free herself.

What is a realistic expectation? If we say to you, "Can you do such and such for us?" Then you say, "Sure, how would you like it done?" We respond, "Like this and this and this." You say, "I can't quite do it that way, but how about this way?" We say, "Okay, that sounds pretty good." Now you know precisely what we want, and we know precisely what you are going to do. That is a realistic expectation. Anything else is unrealistic.

How often do we bump into unrealistic expectations? Any relationship we have could use improved communications. Many of us have the fine fortune of having friends with whom we communicate well. But we cannot take this blessing for granted. We need to work at insuring those relationships. It is hard to maintain open and honest communications. Why? Because we are very often afraid of being rejected. We are afraid of being ourselves because that is being vulnerable.

And being vulnerable is downright scary.

VULNERABILITY AND FEAR OF REJECTION ARE TWO MAIN BARRIERS BLOCKING OUR ABILITY TO RELEASE GUILT. IF WE ARE AFRAID OF BEING VULNERABLE, IT IS BECAUSE WE ARE AFRAID OF BEING REJECTED.

Where does rejection come from originally?
Guess.
It is not just from Mom and Dad; it's from the whole

"growing up" thing. Now, looking back as an adult, we hope that we can say, "Yes, my parents loved me very much." However, when we were little and living it, we may have had our doubts about that love at times. Most of us can look back and agree that our parents loved us. But when we were six years old, it may not have felt that way at times. And for some, tragically, it may not have felt that way ever, because of an abusive relationship.

When you say that someone is feeling guilty about *not* feeling guilty, you can say, "That person was hurt so much that he or she cannot permit vulnerability." It may be so deep a hurt that he or she does not even know what being vulnerable really is anymore. And that person may not know who he or she really is, in relation to other people.

What is on the other side of that wall of guilt and fear? For one thing, freedom from guilt allows us to feel good about ourselves. We have a much clearer self-image. What is on the other side of guilt is being able to communicate more openly in a relationship. What is on the other side is being part of a relationship of any kind without destroying that relationship and without being destroyed in that relationship by guilt and manipulation.

TRUST

If you feel someone has violated your trust, and you feel awful, you want that person to know he has violated your trust, and you want *him* to feel *guilty,* don't you? You want her to know that she hurt you. And by making her feel guilty, you have the hope that she won't do it again.

Let's look at trust for a moment. When you meet someone, does he or she have to struggle and work to prove trustworthiness? Do you spend years and years assessing how honest and sincere a person is, or do you just accept someone and say that you can trust that person? Do you have the person fill out a thirty-page questionnaire on his or her trustworthiness? No. You usually just trust the person.

And when that person violates that trust, in whatever manner, do you then lay on the guilt? Do you say, "Well, you are going to have to earn my trust again." And does the other person say, "Okay, what do I have to do to earn it back?" And do you say, "I don't know, but I'll let you know when you have earned it again." The other person asks, "Is it a week, six months, ten years? What do I have to do to flagellate myself?" And you say, "I don't know."

Why don't you know? Because you didn't know what motivated your trust in the first place.

How and why do you give trust so freely? Even people who normally don't extend trust easily, do it freely. You do because you want to. Why do you want to? Because you want the trust returned. You give something because you want it extended back to you. In short, you treat other people as you want to be treated.

Why, when you feel that your trust was violated, don't you give it back? When you give your trust you are setting yourself up. You are becoming vulnerable. That means that when you trust someone—herein lies the head trip—*the first thing that you do is to set up expectations for yourself and for the relationship.*

Now, when you decide to trust someone, you usually don't sit down together and say to that person, "Look, I trust you, and here are the limits of my trust. How do you feel about those limits? This is the width and breadth of my trust. How do you feel about that?" Likewise, the other person probably doesn't say, "Well, these are my fears and this is who I am. . . ." Hardly. It would be nice, but very unlikely.

Human beings seldom do this. As a result, we have expectations about relationships that are unrealistic. When we give our trust freely, it is our responsibility to communicate with the other person so that our mutual expectations are realistic. I trust you and therefore I am going to talk with you. And in that talking, we will find out who we are. Our expectations of each other will no longer be unrealistic. We won't try to control each other. We will not lay guilt trips on each other.

Why do we seemingly need guilt? We believe that it keeps us safe. Yet, it is not armor. A defense mechanism is armor. Guilt is a weapon.

Could one reason that a mother subconsciously imposes guilt on her children be the fear that her children will no longer need her one day? Is this pattern beginning to sound familiar? Does she hope that by imposing enough guilt, those children will be dependent on her for the rest of their lives? That the children won't be able to put on their slippers without checking with her first?

The weapon is guilt. It is *not* armor.

Likewise, when one spouse imposes guilt on the other, one reason could be that he or she is saying, "I am terrified of getting this close and I'm terrified that you won't need me anymore."

And perhaps the spouse who feels guilty, whether or not the other person is consciously imposing the guilt, is saying the same thing: "I'm terrified that I am worthless in this relationship."

So the person who uses guilt is afraid of not being valuable, and the person who feels guilt is afraid of not being valuable.

WE ARE CONTROLLED BY OUR "GUILT"-
EDGED FEARS.

It all comes back to our self-esteem, our confidence, and our self-image. Trust that is freely given is the only kind of trust that there is. That is why it is so hard to give it back when it has been violated. Therefore, when you feel that your trust has been violated, you still must make the intuitive decision to continue to trust or not to trust.

If you trusted someone once and that person has done something that hurt you, how do you feel that trust again if you decide to? You talk about it. You describe the hurt in a way that isn't being brutally honest. You get feedback. If the other person doesn't want to talk, try telling him or her how important it is. If that person is willing to talk and work it out, you'll discover inside that the trust is right back, just where it was. Forcing the other person to *earn* your trust is a coward's way of saying, "I never wanted to get close to you in the first place, and I ended up getting close; and it hurt. I am never getting close again. Ever!" Now you are controlled by the irrational fear that all closeness will result in violated trust or pain. If you don't take some interpersonal risks, you're completely out of control, since the rest of the world dictates your feelings.

RELEASING GUILT

To release guilt, we have to be willing to feel good about ourselves, but not by attacking other people. We look to the goal of healthier relationships which are happier for everyone involved.

> GUILT DOES NOT EXIST WHERE GOOD
> COMMUNICATION EXISTS. IT JUST SIMPLY
> DOES NOT.

If you examine the situations where another person was blatantly guilt-tripping you, you can usually find poor communication. Poor communication is alive and festering in such relationships. However, when we can acknowledge *self-imposed* guilt, we oftentimes go right back to parental disapproval.

What is the problem in communication with ghosts? How can we begin to sort out the ghostly guilts and the guilty ghosts?

The issue is that parental disapproval occurred when we were children. Now, as adults, we are still trying to get the approval from parents *that existed when we were that age*.

Their approval or disapproval didn't just happen. We were *trained* for their approval or disapproval. We had no choice. Our parents raised us to seek it. Sure, they did their best, but when you are in training, you don't have much to say about it. In addition, the parent is like God to a small child. The child is dependent on the parent. As adults, if we don't like what the instructor in a class teaches, we can manage to struggle through it for three or four months and then it's over. Or we can drop the course and leave right away. When we are children, and our parents say something, it becomes gospel truth for the rest of our lives—or until we let it go. In addition to parental disapproval, long-term effects often exist when a significant other person in our life has left his or her mark on us, through the weapons of guilt and fear.

We have a friend who, at the age of forty-four, has just

begun to wear long, dangly earrings—brightly colored parrots, wildcats, fish, dolphins—that hang halfway down to her shoulders. Sometimes she wears two different earrings (and looks like a walking zoo). Yet, she receives quite a few compliments and has actually met a few new friends that way. It took her until this age to realize that she would not be an instant slut for wearing those earrings, and that her parents, who are dead, would not criticize her. In fact, they might even have liked the colorful, unusual jewelry on a forty-eight-year-old woman, even though they didn't approve of it on their twelve-year-old child in the year 1958.

There is no choice involved, when the overlay upon us is that we are bad, or that we do things that disappoint another. This combined with our fear of rejection means we have been trained to be set up. We must realize that this was done by other people coming from *their* position of fear—fear of losing control, fear of rejection, fear that we would grow up to be "bad," or fear that we would not need them anymore.

In Chapter 4, you will meet Marcy and her mom. Marcy is a grown woman with two small children. When Marcy occasionally asks her mom to baby-sit, in spite of the fact that her mother appears to enjoy having the quality time with her grandchildren, her mom makes her feel guilty in return. Why does Mom do this? Why does Marcy feel the guilt? To understand the answers, we need to ask some more questions.

What do we say to the children who, almost overnight, become independent, after we have spent years preparing them for independence? We took care of them, we loved them, we did our best to prepare them for life, and we tried to encourage them to feel good about themselves.

Do we then say, "Oh, adios, give me a call sometime.

. . . We'll do lunch.'' If you can do that, you either don't love that child or you are the most intact parent on this planet. You see, we prepared them, but we forgot to prepare ourselves.

> THE GREATER THE DEGREE OF OUR OWN INSECURITY OR THE POORER OUR OWN SELF-IMAGE, THE GREATER WILL BE OUR ATTEMPT TO HANG ON TO OUR CHILDREN.

You are the bows from which your children as living arrows are sent forth.

The Archer sees the mark upon the path of the infinite, and He bends you with His might that His arrows may go swift and far.

Let your bending in the Archer's hand be for gladness;

For even as He loves the arrow that flies, so He loves also the bow that is stable.

(Kahlil Gibran, *The Prophet*. New York: Alfred A. Knopf, 1923.)

How do we communicate with, and neutralize, the ghosts of our past? First, we need to recognize the problem for what it is, and how it influences us today. We need to examine those areas in which we feel controlled by guilt from a ghost. Just plain awareness of those areas allows us the freedom to explore.

Do you feel guilty when you are late? Why?

Do you feel guilty when you eat a whole pound of chocolate candy in one afternoon? Why?

Do you feel guilty when your house is messy and dirty? Why?

Do you feel guilty when you cry? Why?

Do you feel guilty when you work eighty hours a week? Why?

Do you feel guilty when you *don't* work eighty hours a week? Why?

Can you make up your own list of those things that automatically make you feel guilty, even when there is no one around to try to make you feel guilty about them? Do you feel guilty about not making the list? Why?

The following true case history came to our attention and indicates how significantly guilt can interfere with someone's performance.

GUILTY AS SIN

Phyllis first started seeing a counselor in March. She was a thirty-six-year-old graduate student, finishing up her dissertation. She indicated that she was happily married, and had three children—two daughters, eight and ten, and a thirteen-year-old son. She had married her college sweetheart, right after graduation. He was employed as a high school teacher. She promptly had the children and stayed home to raise them. She had never been able to find a job utilizing her English degree. Three years ago, she and her husband decided it would be a great idea for her to return to school and to obtain a graduate degree in counseling, specifically adolescent psychology. She had finished her course work, but needed to do additional work on her dissertation. This task she found impossible to do. She only had about fifty pages more to write, yet this requirement was overwhelming to her. If she couldn't get her dissertation done, she couldn't graduate that June.

She admitted to being unable to concentrate. She had writer's block. She felt stressed, depressed, and defensive. She was annoyed with her husband, her kids, her great Aunt Rosie, and the chairman of her committee. In short, she was angry with the significant other people in her environment: her family and her ''boss'' (the person responsible for overseeing her graduate studies).

The counselor asked her why she was angry at her children. It turned out she was mainly annoyed with her son. She had had to go to Seattle suddenly for a week, and while she was gone, her son had gotten mixed up with a rowdy group of kids and run straight into trouble with the police. Her son and several other boys had cut school to visit the local adult porn movie house. While they were there, the place caught fire. The boys were held for truancy and suspected arson. Although it turned out eventually that the fire was due to a short in the wiring in the projector, Phyllis had her fill of police, lawyers, and juvenile hall. Her son was still grounded.

She admitted to being wrapped up in fear and guilt, especially guilt. She knew if she had been home, none of this would have happened. She felt doubly guilty because she had been away over her son's birthday.

The counselor asked her why she was angry at her Aunt Rosie. It turned out that Aunt Rosie was the reason why Phyllis had had to go out of town in the first place. Aunt Rosie was the elderly only sibling of Phyllis's deceased mother, and Phyllis felt responsible for her. Aunt Rosie had never married. Phyllis had planned to visit her in Seattle for a few days during winter break, but the whole family ended up with the flu and she had to postpone the trip. Then in February she received a phone call from Aunt Rosie's attorney. Aunt Rosie had been swindled in a sophisticated con operation. Aunt Rosie had lost half her life savings and had signed over promissory notes for the rest. When Aunt Rosie discovered what had happened, she had a mild heart attack and ended up in the hospital. Phyllis flew immediately to Seattle to see her. Then she had to meet with the police and Rosie's attorney. Phyllis saw her share of police and attorneys in Seattle, too, before she could get the swindle straightened out.

Phyllis told the counselor that she felt guilty about Aunt Rosie. She was responsible for her. If she had gone to Seattle for a few days over the holidays, she felt none of this would have happened: Aunt Rosie wouldn't have been robbed, or been upset enough to have a heart attack.

The counselor inquired why Phyllis was angry at her committee chairman. She replied that he wanted her to write more, to make it an exceptional dissertation. But she now had developed writer's block and couldn't write one more word.

The counselor finally wanted to know why she was upset with her husband. Phyllis said that they had spent quite a lot of money putting her through graduate school. She felt she had not carried her own weight financially in the marriage. She was feeling guilty over this. She felt she couldn't even look for a job in adolescent counseling, since she couldn't even manage her own son. In short, Phyllis had gotten herself so wrapped up in guilt that she was dysfunctional and downright nonfunctional when it came to finishing her dissertation.

Can you, the reader, see how the above spiral of guilt got started and continued to pick up steam until Phyllis could not write one more word on her dissertation? Maybe Phyllis was dysfunctional temporarily for a purpose: to heal from the enormous amount of stress she had been under. She was trying to be everything to everyone: superwoman, supermom, superwife, superniece, superstudent, etc. She was not flowing, flexible Phyllis. She was frozen, fixated Phyllis. She rebelled by saying, in effect, no more.

Can you see how Phyllis needed to neutralize the guilt she was feeling? Through counseling, she came to realize that she would have made the same choices even if she had been a different person. She could not have prevented Aunt Rosie from being swindled unless she had had the possible, but impractical, foresight to hire a Pinkerton guard to keep track of her twenty-four hours a day. And her son would probably have gotten into mischief by caving into raw peer pressure, whether she had gone out of town or not. She realized, finally, that the situation with her son would give her invaluable experience and compassion, not to mention the contacts in the juvenile justice system to allow her to pursue her career in helping troubled adolescents.

Through counseling, Phyllis got out from under the unrealistic expectations she had for herself. She neutralized the guilt that was close to crushing her. She finished up her dissertation and graduated with her class in June. She found a job working for the county.

The above case history shows how it is possible to manipulate ourselves using guilt. As you recognize guilt within yourself and guilt as a weapon of the manipulator, you will be able to see guilt working in the lives of those around you. Some people have almost no self-imposed guilt; others have a great deal. Some people have almost none in certain areas but make up for it big time in others.

When you examine guilt, you need to make it tangible. It may have ghostly qualities and be based on non-reality, but find it, label it, and examine it. Most people keep a little bit of guilt anyway, and use it to form the basis of conscience, to keep themselves from doing things that could hurt others. As with fear (explored in the next chapter), a little bit is okay. As Lew (one of our friends) stated: "You need a little fear in wartime. If you don't have some healthy fear, you'll not come back. It has nothing to do with love. You can love your country, your family, your unit. But without some fear, you're an egomaniac and chances are less that you'll return." And that's what this is about. Returning. Surviving. Neutralizing. Succeeding. In war and in peace.

CHAPTER 3

Fear

One of the Two Major Weapons of the Manipulator

I freak out at the thought of spiders . . . great big hairy spiders. The thought of squashing something like that makes my skin crawl. I was in Israel in 1971 and living on a kibbutz in the Negev Desert. There are lots of strange creatures in the desert. I was on kitchen cleanup one morning about 3:00 A.M., and a spider the size of a shoe box walked in. This spider just sauntered into the kitchen, with its sixteen thousand eyes and eight translucent legs. Now, if this had been a fox or a bobcat, I might have treated it with respect and tossed it a few scraps, but it wasn't. I froze. I was up on a ladder. A kibbutznik was slicing potatoes on the cutting board. He looked over, saw this spider-from-hell and carefully dropped the cutting board on top of it, then stepped on it. The best part was that after this, he just picked up the cutting board and went back to work. Most people cannot do this.   —DR. GREEN

THE IRONY:
FEELING FEARFUL ABOUT LETTING GO OF FEAR

When therapists work with clients who are beset with fear, they often discover that the clients fear letting go of their fears. They face the battle of the "what-if's." Let's use the above example of spiders.

If we told you that you could be hypnotized so that you would no longer be afraid of spiders, you might not want to get rid of that fear. Think about that for a minute. No matter how much you believed in the therapist, or in the power of hypnosis, you might not want to love spiders. If you could become so "up" that the highlight of your day is kissing the back of your pet tarantula, would you really want to imagine this? You'd probably say, "Uh . . . don't do me any favors. Hypnotize me to lose weight, but leave the spiders out of it!" Why is that? It's the fear of letting go of a fear.

It is extremely difficult to conceptualize what is on the other side of that wall of fear. Just as with guilt.

RELEASING FEAR

To release fear, we have to be willing to feel good about ourselves, but not by attacking other people. We look to the goal of healthier relationships that are happier for everyone involved.

Let's look at fear. How many of us live in fear? All of us. Constantly. Fear of everything from earthquakes to the salt of the earth, toxic waste to body odor. Fear of ourselves.

Fear can easily be placed side by side with guilt, as weapons of the manipulator. Do you have any specific fears? Ones that can be used against you by any average manipulator? If you can identify them, it will be of significant help to you in countering manipulation.

Can you make up a list of your fears? Like the guilt list

in the last chapter? And then check it against the following more common fears:

Fear of embarrassment or humiliation.

Fear of losing one's status (job, relationships, approval of others).

Fear of having a definition of reality that is not shared by others.

Fear of losing another person who means a lot to you.

Fear of being hurt by violence in our society.

Fear of loss of material possessions.

Fear of nuclear war.

Fear of a specific group of people.

Fear of floods, fires, and other natural disasters.

Fear of riots.

Fear of hurting another person unintentionally.

Being aware of the fears on your list and the guilts on your other list will make it easier eventually to release them. Then, they can no longer be used effectively against you as weapons by the manipulator. You can afford vulnerability; you can trust again, and you open up communication confident that you can neutralize future attempts by others to manipulate you.

Fear can be a funny thing. As a matter of fact, if you fear mathematics, you may want to skip down two paragraphs. Fear as a formula is expressed as $F = 3x - 2y +$ the square root of z. Fear = three times the amount of sweat in your armpits (x), minus twice the knots in the pit of your stomach (y), plus the square root of the reality of the situation (z). If you are waist deep in floodwaters (z) or someone is holding a gun on you (z), you can readily observe that fear (F) will have a relatively high value. Lots of real white-knuckle fear.

On the other hand, if the reality of the situation (z) is not up to your fantasy and worry about the situation, you will end up with a *negative* value for the reality of the situation (z). And the square root of z will be the square root of a negative number and will, therefore, be an *imaginary number.* This is the long way around of stating that fear can be examined in depth, like guilt. We can look at fear in its many tangible aspects as well as its ghostly aspects.

Getting fear out of the way in verbal manipulative situations is what we aim to do utilizing the model of the soft martial arts. How often is the martial artist in a movie portrayed as a cowering wimp? Not often. How many Teenage Mutant Ninja Turtles or Power Rangers are belly-up by the end of the show? Not many. One of the philosophies behind the martial arts says: You are powerful, you are alert, you are the one in control. The attack is *not* personal, except in the sense that you are viewed by someone else as having more power and strength, or you would not have been attacked in the first place. The old saying goes something like this: Only the rigid oak tree breaks in the storm; the flexible willow bends. You flow with the energy. You use the inherent weaker power of your attacker to defeat him or her, not *your* energy. Use the attackers' power to defeat them. Through holds, immobilization, and locks, the attackers end up controlled by the very same negative energy they tried to slam on you.

The martial artist learns early on that his own fears will operate against him if he does not learn to stop investing energy in them and let them go. The training for his or her belt or rank is dependent on learning the skills and learning about the self, so that in an attack situation, no weakness will be apparent that could be used against the martial artist by the enemy.

Besides guilt to battle, we have both internal and external fears to face. Each of our characters presented in the next chapter has fear operating in his or her situation, not to mention an ample dose of guilt.

Archie is terrified of his own debilitating disability and hence attacks everyone in sight to take his mind off his impending mortality. Sheila fears the implied threat inherent in all sexual harassment. Fred fears looking like a fool in front of guests and employees in a resort hotel. He's also not thrilled by the implication of a comment that he's on death's doorstep. The department store insists Carlos be polite to customers. Unfortunately, the people who come in are not given the same instructions. These dissatisfied customers approach Carlos with huge chips on their shoulders and treat him as if he manufactured products himself. When someone starts yelling at us, we usually tend to tense with fear. Anger comes later.

Nancy the nurse and Dave, who works for a slave-driving employer, both live under the umbrella of fear that they might lose their jobs. And while Nancy would love to tell a demanding patient, "Touch that buzzer one more time and you'll be back in the emergency room," she can't. She knows that no matter what she does, the patient is just waiting for any excuse to pick up the phone, call the hospital administrator, and then his or her attorney. Likewise, Dave instinctively fears that mouthing off to his boss is a gamble he can't risk.

Annie the airhead, Tess the preteen, and Martin are basically in social situations, not employer, family, or spouse situations. The only power that the tormenters have over them is the power they themselves give up. If they neutralize the manipulations, the craziness should stop. The manipulators, after all, are really trying, *and successfully,* to reduce Annie's, Tess's, and Martin's self-image.

THINKING ABOUT PARENTS

The conflict of Marcy and her mom over the occasional baby-sitting has the least fear involved. Mostly governed by guilt, Marcy falls into the category of grown-up child. "Once a child, always a child" rules many a household. Marcy was dependent on Mom for a long time, as most infants and young children are. Now she is independent. The role of adult to adult takes some getting used to. Any fear that Marcy has would be left over from the "Honor thy mother and father" concept instilled in her from infancy. To tell her mother that her behavior is driving Marcy crazy could be interpreted as a lack of respect. Her mother, on the other hand, is experiencing the substantial fear of loss of value as a parent.

Any discussion of manipulation always brings out the classic question: How can you teach your children without using guilt and fear? More specifically, how can you convey the severity of the dangers out there in the world without using fear?

First of all, it is the parent's fear that is being injected into the child, isn't it? Let's take the example of teaching your five-year-old how to cross a busy intersection. Up to this point, the child has not been allowed out of the yard. Up to this point, the child has viewed crossing that intersection as a challenge. The child visualizes dodging between the cars without tangling with a steamroller and ending up looking like a large, thin pizza lying in the middle of the road. But if that should happen, the child will spring back to life anyway, just like in the cartoons. Without scaring the wits out of the child, what can you do? Are you coming from your own insecurity? Are control and power your motivations? Let's say no to both questions and continue:

My father taught me to look both ways. What the green light meant and what the red light meant. What the yellow light meant. What W-A-L-K stood for and what D-O-N-T W-A-L-K meant. He taught me how to make eye contact with the drivers nearby. And how when the cars were stopped, to proceed carefully and directly across the intersection. He instructed me in crossing that street. Then my parents tested me by allowing me to cross the street under their supervision. And do you know what? When they were all done, my mom typed up this little three-by-five card as a street crossing license that I carried in my pocket for the next two years. They told me to carry it in case someone stopped me to see if I was allowed to cross the street. I still have that "license."

—DR. GREEN

Love and concern are the means of teaching a child or an individual the art of self-preservation. Yet, we can only teach children the best way we know how, and sometimes it's pretty lame. For example, we can work our hardest to teach our kindergarten-age children not to accept rides from strangers. One way is to make a game where anyone but Mom or Dad or Grandma trying to pick up Joey or Jan at school must know the secret password. This creates fun without detailing kidnapping, rape, and murder as the alternative. But then you'll forget all about the password, and two years later all hell will break loose at school. You forgot to give Aunt Patti from out of town the password, and Joey goes screaming off his face for the police when she tries to cram him in the car.

Children aren't stupid either. They witness so much violence in our society, in their own backyards, in their own schools. Fear is rampant. Many children sit spellbound in front of violent videos. Do they think if they watch enough of this, it'll serve as an inoculation against violence in their own lives? See enough fear and face it on the TV and you can deal with any situation? Not likely.

In a world of disease, war, famine, riots, and natural
disasters, it becomes almost silly to rant and rave over issues such as "Eat your carrots, or you'll go blind. Pick
your belly button, and your fanny will fall off. Straighten
your room, or you're grounded for a month." Your teen
looks at you and blinks twice. His friend Johnny just got
grounded for a month for cutting classes. "What . . . not
cleaning my room warrants . . . grounding?"

Trying to inculcate fear into children, for the most part
your own fear, can backfire, and you can get nailed right
on the spot. Consider the little boy in the following true
example:

It was the Saturday before Christmas, and my ten-
year-old son and I were shopping at the huge local
mall. There were tens of thousands of shoppers shov-
ing their way in and out of stores that day. I was
stressed and, quite frankly, not in the spirit of the
holidays. Suddenly, my son spotted a holiday display.
A big sleigh filled with presents with a life-size ani-
mated reindeer. The reindeer nodded its head up and
down and from side to side. However, this docile deer
sported a pair of antlers that could have impaled
Santa himself. My son broke rank and rushed over,
leaving me to fight my own way through the large
crowd encircling Rudolph. In truly manipulative fashion, my own power base near zero, I hollered,
"Watch out for those antlers." My son shot me a
withering look that indicated I should get a life for
myself. Then he slowly smiled. He stepped up to Rudolph, and leaned forward. Suddenly, he reeled backward, slapped both hands over his left eye, and started
screaming at the top of his lungs, "My eye, my eye."
A collective gasp rose from the crowd. Someone

yelled, "Call 911!" I grabbed my grinning son and left the mall in great haste. —ANONYMOUS PARENT

In this case, the young boy made the fantasy *really* real. He was no baby. Having his eye poked out by Rudolph wasn't high on his wish list. He didn't plan on spending Christmas vacation in the pediatric wing. He didn't like the implication that Mom thought he was so stupid that he didn't recognize the danger. On top of that Mom had to announce it to a large group of people. Why did she have to bring it up? Her own fear is why. Never mind that Mom had had to take the boy to the doctor twice during the past week. It wasn't his fault that the strange dog bit him in the park. And it could have been anyone in the free-for-all on the school bus who later needed stitches.

Fear can be so internalized that it takes years to show up. Your brain has powerful protective resources. You may experience a particular fear only as a peculiar discomfort that makes no sense at all. Examples are endless and can be attested to by counselors and psychologists. Most of us lead our entire lives without realizing all the reasons for our idiosyncrasies. Other times fears emerge with or without encouragement, as in the case of flashbacks that appear out of nowhere.

The following events happened to a friend and illustrate how great the grip fear can have on someone, even from the grave.

THE STAMP AND THE ENVELOPE

At the time she sought counseling, Susan was a forty-three-year-old part-time receptionist in a dentist's office. She was satisfied with her job. She was married and had three children, two boys and a girl, all in their teens. She had been married once before, briefly, at age nineteen, and got divorced at twenty-two, with no children from that marriage. She was an only child. Both her parents were dead. They had died eighteen months prior, within four months of each other, each having suffered from Alzheimer's. Susan had helped care for them. Susan was suffering from enormous stress and had Jungian-type nightmares (black skeletons on black stallions, etc.). She also admitted feeling a great deal of anxiety, or nameless terror as she described it. She indicated it was becoming increasingly difficult for her to concentrate at work. Even down to the point where she couldn't remember on which side of the envelope to place the stamp. The therapist's immediate intervention helped her deal with stress along with grief counseling.

It was apparent to the counselor that Susan was suffering from an enormous fear of death, to the point of being phobic. While she admitted it was silly, Susan was badly distracted by her need to become immortal.

The counselor explored various areas of Susan's life, looking for other fears. In the counseling relationship, they found quite a few normal fears, explained away by logical cause and effect. For instance, Susan was terrified of driving with her teenage daughter, who had just gotten her learner's permit. In the course of therapy, it turned out that she and her daughter had had a most unpleasant driving experience when her daughter was five years old and they were living overseas. They had gone to an amusement park. Not a regulated, licensed, inspected kind of place. Unbeknownst to the family, one had to be sixteen to drive these bumper cars from the Indy 500. The attendant was not paying attention, and the ride started with Susan's five-year-old at the wheel. To make a long story short, in Susan's desperate attempt to pull her daughter from behind the wheel, they crashed. Both ended up in the local emergency room with fairly severe injuries.

This helped to explain why they were uptight with the present driving situation. Once her daughter became licensed, Susan could see how she would be free to enjoy riding with her daughter. Once the state showed that it considered her daughter a competent driver by granting her a driver's license, Susan did not feel as much responsibility to protect her.

Over the course of the next month, she overcame other specific fears. However, she still had a phobia about death and was truly a woman on a mission to cheat death at any cost. On the surface, Susan admitted it was ridiculous, but it still interfered with her concentration and relaxation. Then the family cat died. The cat had belonged to her parents, and Susan's family had inherited him. Susan slipped back into the night terrors, waking up everyone in the house.

Further along in counseling, Susan volunteered information about her parents, especially how they related to her as a teenager. Her mother was a kind, compassionate woman who had given up a law practice to stay home and raise Susan, since that's what a lot of women felt they had to do in those days. She could tell her mother virtually anything, and it would go no further. Her mother played a game where she wasn't her mother and would listen like the wise old woman in Joseph Campbell's hero journey, occasionally advise her, never punish her.

Her father worked for the government. He was good-humored also, but he was terrified that something would happen to Susan. She had been born the only child to her parents when they were both forty years old. They couldn't "make" another Susan if something should happen to her, so her father became obsessed with protecting her. She couldn't even cut her own apple; he'd do it for her—he was afraid she'd cut her fingers off. She couldn't lick her own postage stamps because of his fear (!!!)—he was afraid she'd lick them too hard and they'd fall off. Susan's father was so wrapped up in his own fear of something happening to Susan that he smothered her. He frequently threatened to kill himself if she got pregnant, got arrested, or flunked out of school. "Life won't be worth living," he'd say. "I'll just die if you get arrested." "I'll kill myself if you get pregnant or flunk out of school." Although attractive, she never dated. And she got straight A's.

Through counseling, Susan quickly realized that her father's love for her, overprotective as it was, had put her in a double bind. As long as he was alive, and she didn't get arrested, flunk out of school, or get pregnant out of holy matrimony, his implied promise was that he would *stay* alive. However, when he died, Susan believed, at least on the subconscious level, that she must have done something very wrong or he would still be alive. She was bearing the full responsibility for his death. She was very frightened for him and for herself.

Can you, as the reader, see how Susan might become so wrapped up in grief and express it, in light of her father's threats, through exaggerated fear?

Susan continued in counseling for a while. Just by identifying the fear made her feel better, but she was far from rebounding instantly. She also mourned the death of the family cat. Her counselor took her through the grief process until she was able to begin seeing death as a logical part of life. Finally, her counselor suggested: "Why not get a new kitten for the family?" Susan did.

We can be manipulated through fear. There are many areas where you will see friends or even family using fear on others. As with guilt, you can make fear tangible and consider both the real and non-real aspects of it. You can label it, and maybe even keep a little bit of it. If we had no fear, no guilt, who could we be?

Let's look at the Five Levels for neutralizing manipulation, beginning with the next chapter.

CHAPTER 4

Hear No Evil:
Level One

"Friday, I think you have missed the most alarming symptom of all."

"I have? Are you going to tell me?". ...

"Mmm. This once I shall tell you. . . . Sick cultures show a complex of symptoms such as you have named [Violence. Muggings. Sniping. Arson. Bombing. Terrorism . . . Riots. . . .] but a *dying* culture invariably exhibits personal rudeness. Bad manners. Lack of consideration for others in minor matters. A loss of politeness, of gentle manners, is more significant than a riot." (ROBERT HEINLEIN)

We are far from living in The Thousand Years of the Greatest Peace the World Has Ever Known. Living in a world that oftentimes seems out of control affects us and those around us. When people try to compensate for their own feelings of hopelessness by attempting to control their environment, they often try to control other people along with it. Hence, manipulation becomes even more prevalent. Hence, you may see even more "compliments" coming your way.

The system presented here contains only five easy-to-implement levels for countering manipulation. Level One is the most gentle. Level Five is the most severe. When using the five techniques, it's wise to use the lowest level possible to accomplish your purpose: neutralizing the manipulator and ending the manipulation.

Like the martial artist, you need to change the rules of the game, so that the manipulators no longer succeed. The manipulators will then be forced to play using your rules. Ideally, when you successfully counter a manipulation, the manipulative energy will be neutralized. The manipulator ends up holding the full force of his or her *own* negative energy that went into the attack (manipulation) in the first place. You have taken none of the negative energy. You will learn to use the right level to neutralize these manipulations. You don't want to do a takedown and slam others to the mat when they've just tapped you on the shoulder to ask directions. It's a waste of energy to overreact.

Of course, at this point you are wondering, Why not just ask the persons who offend me to stop doing whatever they are doing? Most manipulators have a standard answer when asked the question, "Why are you trying to manipulate me?" or "Why are you trying to make me feel guilty?" They will respond with: "Doing *what?*" When dealing with manipulators, you can temporarily kiss logic goodbye.

In most manipulations, there exists an inherent dare to the person being manipulated. The manipulators want you to buy into their game, using *their* rules. If you challenge them using *their* rules, they have you where they want you. Challenging them about a manipulative attempt will only bring on a greater attack. With or without awareness of what they are doing, the manipulators will deny that they are manipulating, and paint *you* into the crazy corner. Or, they will openly point out your fear or guilt for all the world to see, using brutal honesty (this will be addressed in Chapter 9). They will get you so angry that you wind up saying or doing something stupid that will get you hurt or fired, or becoming so wrapped up in guilt that you voluntarily submit to being manipulated.

Please realize at this point that most manipulations occur at the subconscious level, or at the very least at a low conscious level. No one, unless they are malicious, says, "Okay, it's Thursday, time to go manipulate Joyce for a while."

We will now introduce ten characters, drawn from real life. Their particular situations come directly from Dr. Green's clinical practice and the observations of the authors. These characters will illustrate how to use the five different levels of countering manipulation. They come from many different backgrounds, with the manipulative attempts occurring in their families, in their workplaces, in their social interactions, as well as in one-shot deals. Almost certainly, you will be able to relate to at least one of these characters, and probably to several of them.

You will readily recognize that in certain situations, one or more levels of countering manipulation may be inappropriate to use. However, each level's techniques will be explored, so that you end up feeling confident and comfortable operating on all five levels in your own particular situation.

DO YOU KNOW
DAVE WHO WORKS FOR ATTILA THE HUN?

Dave is an excellent employee doing a decent job. He holds an entry-level management position and has hopes of moving up the corporate ladder. His boss, nicknamed Attila the Hun by those in the department, recognizes Dave's outstanding capabilities. However, he repeatedly gives Dave more work than can possibly be done by the assigned deadline. Up until now, Dave has managed (barely) to get the work done each time by staying overtime, or by taking work home. This frustrates Attila even more. One morning he calls Dave into his office and says, "I need these reports for Acme Corporation by noon today." Dave blinks twice as he looks at a whole week's worth of work to do in four hours. How does Dave counter this situation so, hopefully, it won't continue?

AND HERE'S
ANNIE THE AIRHEAD

Annie likes to dress up really, really, cute. She looks like she is fourteen years old, although she is twenty-nine. She even puts pink bows in her hair. She does it because she likes what she sees in the mirror. And she makes it work. Her appearance gives another definition to the word "cute." But because of her cuteness, she has been a constant object of ridicule in her office. She is treated like an airhead even though she is an extremely competent employee. Finally, one day when she thinks that she just can't take it anymore, a co-worker comes up and says, "Hey, Annie, how many Annies does it take to change a light bulb?" How does Annie respond?

YOU'VE COME ACROSS
CARLOS THE CUSTOMER SERVICE
REPRESENTATIVE

Carlos meets a lot of manipulative people at the complaint desk.

Can you imagine what it would be like to work there, assuming that you aren't already working there, which may be one reason that you're reading this book. Do you ever wonder how long it takes before someone gets totally discouraged? Do you wonder what the average job tenure is? Hours, days, weeks, months?

DID YOU FIND
FRED THE FRONT DESK MANAGER?

Fred is the front desk manager at a large resort hotel. The lobby near the front desk area is always full, with guests checking in or out. Fred must insure that everything goes smoothly and, above all, that the guests feel welcome. Fred is forty-seven years old with prematurely white hair. He is sensitive about this. It is mid-afternoon, and about forty people are standing around in various lines. One guy near the end of one line tries to get Fred's attention. He sees Fred's name tag and yells, "Fred, yo...." Fred pays no attention to him. The guy yells, "Hey, Fred, how old are you?" Fred can't be rude to this guy. Fred answers, "Forty-seven." More than several dozen people and more than several employees are listening at this point. The guy comes back with, "I never knew a guy named Fred to live past the age of fifty!" How does Fred counter or neutralize this?

PLEASE MEET
MARCY AND HER MOM

Marcy is a grown woman with two young children. Her mother lives in the same city and appears to take a great deal of delight in being asked to baby-sit her grandchildren occasionally. Marcy's parents are both retired, and her mom is always saying how bored silly she is. Marcy views this as a golden opportunity for her children to have quality time with their grandparents. But her mother has one unnerving characteristic. Every time Marcy asks her to watch the children, her mother replies like this: "Your dad and I would be happy to, however that evening is the *only* evening your dad and I have to be alone together for the next month [this is simply untrue, and Marcy knows it]; but that's fine, we'll cancel our plans, we'd love to sit the children." Or, "That is the one afternoon this year that your dad and I had wanted to go to the movies together. But that's okay, we're more than happy to watch the kids." Each time this happens, Marcy feels guilty for the next three days.

Remember, Mom really does like watching the kids occasionally. How can Marcy handle this persistent manipulation and still maintain a great relationship with her mother?

MAYBE YOU'VE MET
MARTIN THE CLUB MEMBER?

Clara has a habit of shooting people down in public, with everything from rude insults to something trivial. Then she hunts down the offended individual in private and apologizes (the Closet Apologizer). The victims usually end up accepting the apology, which then sets them up for the next round. Clara and Martin are members of a group or club; we'll say "The Group." At their monthly meeting, in front of everyone, Martin says, "Hey, Clara, I saw you downtown this morning. I honked and waved, but you didn't see me." To which Clara replies, "I wasn't downtown this morning."

Martin, says, "Hey, I know it was you, Clara. I know

your car, your special license plate, AGROUP, and you."
To which Clara replies, "You must be crazy. It couldn't
have been me. I was digging up tulip bulbs this morning."
Martin stops this interaction because he feels too stupid to
continue. On the next break, Clara catches Martin at the
water fountain, out of earshot of the others, and says, "Hey,
I'm sorry, I guess it *was* me you saw."

This type of conflict can be played over and over again.
It is a hard one to neutralize unless you realize that it is a
pattern.

HAVE YOU NOTICED
NANCY THE NURSE?

Nancy is an exceptionally conscientious nurse. Because
of her work schedule, she usually has certain specific patients for several days, then has a day off, and upon returning, ends up with a different set of patients. In some
instances, a former patient, whose room Nancy has to walk
by all day long, will want Nancy's attention for any number
of reasons. For example, she treated him better than the
new nurse does, or she looks like his daughter. It is not
appropriate for Nancy to minister to him. He is not her
responsibility, and she, quite frankly, does not have the
time to devote to him. Yet his family is constantly grabbing
Nancy in the hall for small favors. Nancy does not belong
there, but the patient has the unrealistic expectation that she
does. How can she counter this gracefully and get free from
feeling guilty?

YOU MAY TUNE INTO
TESS THE PRETEEN

Tess is having a hard time going through her preteen
years. She is not enjoying the cruel games that some of her

peers play at school. She feels awkward and out of control. In reality, she is a popular young girl with several close friends. She makes good grades and is actively involved in extracurricular activities. Yet hardly a day goes by when she doesn't get taunted by cruel or embarrassing comments. "Hey, Tess, look at Tess, everybody; she has a huge zit on her nose." "Hey, Tess, isn't that the same T-shirt you wore yesterday?" "Hey, Tess, where do you buy your clothes, at the thrift shop?" What does Tess learn to do?

SURELY YOU KNOW
SEXY SHEILA

Sheila had the fortune, or misfortune, of growing up to look like a magazine cover model. She received her master's degree in Business Administration last year. She is on a career path with a large corporation and dresses appropriately for her position. The "wolves" in her department come from all levels of the organization—from several of her employees to several in upper management. Does Sheila have any options in the way of countering the occasional sexual intimidations and insults, short of going to her attorney and filing sexual harassment charges? Hopefully, as increased attention is focused on this specific manipulative behavior in the workplace, fewer and fewer women will be fearful of reporting personal violations.

PLEASE MEET
CATHERINE AND HER COUSIN

Until Catherine got married, she always felt lonesome, being an only child, and dreamed of having a large family. When she met one of her new cousins, she realized how fortunate she had been before. Archie is one of the most insecure people Catherine has ever met. He tries to bully everyone, including little children and the handicapped, even though he has taken early retirement for his own disability. He takes great pride in making fun of most of humanity's higher values. There is not a race or religion that Archie does not hate. There is not a law or leader that Archie admires. There is not one issue on which Archie does not have a vehement negative opinion. No person or thing is immune to Archie's venom. In short, Archie finds no pleasant aspect about life on this planet, and he is going to make sure, before he is through, that no one else will either.

He attacks and manipulates so viciously that his victims may become dysfunctional, while, of course, he becomes high as a kite with power. (Remember the transference of power?) Any reasonable efforts to communicate with him have failed. All subtle efforts by Catherine to end the relationship have failed.

What can Catherine do? She cannot attack Archie, because that is against her nature. She could let him turn his own destructive energy back onto himself, so that he can feel the tremendous power of the anger, fear, and guilt that he continually provokes in others. But will she? What does Catherine do?

In Level One, you give the persons trying to manipulate you the opportunity to correct themselves. In other words, using the martial arts example, someone tries to threaten you but you just turn and walk away. Unaffected. No contest. No fight. Level One is as gentle as it is simple. It is *almost* too simple, but not quite, and it works better than you may initially believe. "Naaaa," you say, "that won't work." As you practice this technique, you will surprise yourself how often it *does* work.

In Level One, you "deaf" the person who is trying to manipulate you. You act as if you are deaf.

EVEN THOUGH THE MANIPULATOR KNOWS THAT ONE MINUTE AGO YOU COULD HEAR JUST FINE, HUMAN NATURE IS SUCH THAT THE MANIPULATOR'S BRAIN WILL RECORD IT AS TRUTH THAT YOU *CANNOT* HEAR AT ALL NOW.

Watch a small child trying to get Mother's attention when Mother does not give it. What does that child do?

"Mommy, I want a cookie." "*Mommy,* I want a cookie." "*Mommy, I want a cookie!!!*" The child speaks louder and louder. The child believes Mommy went deaf all of a sudden and cannot hear her.

Let's look at the customer service/complaint department at a large discount store. The job description for the customer-service representative requires each employee to deal with angry and upset customers in such a way that they will become and remain loyal and happy customers of the store. Even though it appears to be the opposite sometimes, most stores, banks, and services try to keep their customers satisfied. Most do not train their representatives to be card-carrying cads.

So Carlos the Customer Service Representative, works at a large discount department store and sometimes ends up with more than his share of hostility. A customer comes up to him yelling and swearing. "This blender is a piece of *%&$. I don't know why I buy anything here." Of course, there are other customers and employees in the immediate area. Carlos employs Level One. He deafs the angry customer and continues working on some papers. Carlos ignores both the manipulator and his manipulation. He gives the customer an opportunity to correct his socially unacceptable behavior.

This customer will now do one of two things: He will either yell louder and louder, running the risk of drawing a lot of attention to himself (in which case Carlos will move to a higher level of countering manipulation), or he will realize how ridiculous he is sounding and straighten up his act. "I bought this blender, and it fell apart."

Carlos then is no longer deaf and says, "Let me get you a replacement; let me give you your money back; let me exchange it for a better one." Carlos has ignored the inappropriate behavior and has rewarded positive behavior. It's that simple. Carlos has allowed John Doe the choice of calming down and communicating like an adult (Carlos didn't make the blender fall apart) or escalating the confrontation by screaming louder and louder until the customer, himself, looks like an idiot.

In some complaint departments, Carlos, by policy, would not be permitted to use Level One, no matter what. But in this example, Carlos did, and he changed the rules of the game.

The customer wanted nothing better than to make Carlos feel guilty or angry or afraid. Carlos could have come back with the classic reactions that we all know so well: "*Oh, yeah????*" Or, "It is not!" "Is too!" "Is not!" "Is too!"

Another example where Level One can work well is with Dave Who Works for Attila the Hun. Here, the boss keeps giving Dave increasingly unrealistic work loads. Up until now, Dave has managed to get the work done by the deadline by knocking himself silly. Now he is being asked to do a whole week's work in one morning. In real life, Dave actually used Level Four to accomplish his mission. But for the sake of argument, let's say Attila's demands are not limited to Dave.

Late one afternoon, Attila looks over the shoulder of another employee and starts screaming, "Is *that all* you've gotten done?" The employee deafs him. "*I said is that all you've gotten done?!!!*" The employee deafs him again. The boss now has to make a choice whether he will become the center of attention for a whole floor of employees with everyone watching his fit, or become more civil. Attila says, "How's it coming along?" "Fine," says the employee. "Should be done soon."

Let's look at some more of the people we met in the last chapter and see if Level One might be appropriate for them or not. There are times when it is just plain silly or obviously inappropriate to use some of the levels.

Fred, the forty-seven-year-old, white-haired, hotel front desk manager, got slimed by a hotel guest. ("I've never known anyone named Fred to live past the age of fifty.") Fred decided that the guest needed a stronger measure than simply being deafed, although that was one of his options. He decided that this fellow needed to get a dose of his own energy and be stopped once and for all. Continuing this game was not high on Fred's wish list. He opted for Level Five.

Annie the Airhead had tried deafing, but that had not worked. The cruel teasing continued. On to a higher level for Annie.

Marcy and Her Mom experience continuing tension over the baby-sitting issue. Obviously, when Mom starts in with her spiel over the telephone, Marcy's playing deaf is not going to work. "Uh, Marcy, you there? . . . Marcy, where are you? . . . Must have gotten disconnected." So Mom phones back.

Tess the Preteen uses Levels One, Two, or Three primarily. Repeating the same insult three or more times, increasingly louder, puts the other young people squarely in the center of attention. They generally do not wish to be there, and this usually requires more effort than they wish to spend. Level One works a good portion of the time.

Deafing Clara the Closet Apologizer, is not a realistic response. Clara has shot Martin down in public, and in order to neutralize her efforts he needs to come back with something tangible, not just ignore her remarks.

Nancy the Nurse can deaf the demanding patient and his family, but if her supervisor catches her, she will have a lot of explaining to do. Deafing anyone crying out for a drink of water or a pain pill does not reflect well on the hospital's image of "being there because we care."

With Sexy Sheila, Level One can be used on many occasions. "Hey, Sheila, baby," a fellow employee whispers under his breath, "how about a little romp in the broom closet? Boy, would I like to get my hands on your———!" This is not necessarily something that the manipulator wants to yell louder and louder. He may repeat it, but unless Sheila is alone with him, he probably won't shout it out loud. If the manipulator says suggestive things to her in public to embarrass her, then she may need more than deafing—like the phone number of the personnel director or the corporation's attorney. If the harasser is daring her to admit her sexuality in front of others, he may be playing upon her guilt about sex, if she has any. He may be counting on her fear of public embarrassment. Or, he may be trying to get her angry about his invading her privacy. In any event, it is *her* choice to decide when and how she will counter these manipulations effectively.

If Archie, Catherine's cousin, were sensitive enough to tune into Levels One and Two and back off, he would not have people diving for cover when they saw him coming. But, alas, he isn't that sensitive.

Level One is very gentle and can be used anywhere with anyone—family or friends or employees. It implicitly says, "I am bothered by your attempted manipulation of me, and I choose not to reward inappropriate behavior by responding to it on your terms." It says very gently, "I am giving you the opportunity to change your behavior." You have not hurt anyone by extending them the opportunity to approach you in a better, more reasonable way.

Finally, think of the content of Level One in the following example: You are in your place of worship praying. Or, if you prefer, let's say you are sitting alone, meditating, and your eyes are closed. That won't work? Okay, think about lying in a warm bubble bath in your tub. Your head is resting against the back of the tub. Soothing music plays. Your eyes are closed.

Suddenly you are not alone. Suddenly there is terrific noise pollution. Someone is standing there, trying to get your attention. He or she is trying to interrupt you. It is simply not appropriate for this person to be here, doing this. You continue to mind your own business. You keep your eyes and your mouth closed. This is an invasion of your privacy. Now, one of two things will happen. The intruder may recognize that he or she is out of line trying to interrupt you (unless, of course, the building is on fire), say excuse me, and leave. End of encounter.

Or, the intruder will become even more persistent, risking detection by others, along with your possible anger. If this is what the intruder is hoping for, you will surprise him or her, won't you? Because you will move on to Level Two, and that is not what the intruder expected.

The motto for Level One is "I hear you knockin', but there's no one home."

To summarize Level One:

1. Know that the manipulator is "complimenting" you.
2. Know that you are the one with the greater power at this point and deaf the manipulator.
3. If the manipulator backs down and approaches you in a reasonable fashion, the encounter is over.
4. If the manipulator escalates the obnoxious behavior, you know you can move on to higher levels of counteracting the manipulation. You are not a victim.

CHAPTER 5

Speak No Evil:
Level Two

With Level Two, you again give the manipulators the opportunity to clean up their act. Whereas in Level One, you suddenly went deaf to both the manipulation and the manipulator, in Level Two, *you deaf or ignore the manipulations but react in a friendly manner to the manipulators.* You don't act obsequious, merely open and happy to see them. This, in itself, is charming and disarming. Combined with deafing the manipulations, it is quite a powerful tool.

Let's explore this further using our manipulated friends from before. It is right after lunch, and Annie the Airhead is working at her desk. A co-worker, Marge, comes along and makes an anti-airhead comment:

CO-WORKER: "Hey, Annie, have you bought yourself a pink sports car yet?"

She repeats herself three times, while Annie deafs her. (Level One doesn't work, so on to Level Two).

ANNIE (looks up from her desk, smiles sweetly): "Oh, hi, Marge. . . . Great day, huh?"

Now it is up to Marge to decide whether to repeat the remark. Is she going to say, "Yo, Annie, I said [insult number 96]." Possibly she will. But maybe she'll be caught off guard enough to leave it alone or reconsider.

In cases of public put-down or public intimidation, you need to calmly determine where you stand. In continuing relationships, you also need to ask yourself where you are in the pecking order—Is the whole gang manipulating you, or is it just one or two manipulators?

When you witness an encounter where someone is publicly humiliated, how do you react? You probably feel empathy for the person being humiliated. Never underestimate other people's ability to empathize with the slimy feeling when you are the one being attacked.

The opposite circumstance involves the mob mentality, where several people gang up on you and there is not a friendly face in sight. In this case, you are outnumbered and need to be cautious using the higher levels. Ironically, it is better to hold your ground with Level One by deafing both the manipulation and the manipulator. It would take a pretty powerful martial artist to defend himself against numerous assailants at the same time.

Sexy Sheila uses Level Two often. She simply refuses to give the manipulation or the manipulator any of her time or energy:

RUDE RANDY: "I'd sure like to get my hands on your————."

(He repeats himself three times, while Sheila deafs him. Then she goes on to Level Two.)

SHEILA (looks up from her work and flashes a big smile): "Oh, hi, Randy. How're the Acme reports coming along?"

Does Randy start over again at square one? Maybe, maybe not. Remember the martial arts. Sheila has changed the rules and has confused the manipulator. However, if he is persistent enough, this may not work. And Sheila still has the option of reporting Randy for sexual harassment.

Level Two is useful for Carlos, who works at the customer service desk. If Level One didn't calm down the angry customer, it is a natural for Carlos to go to Level Two. Level Two cannot get Carlos into trouble since he is still being friendly, helpful, and professional.

CUSTOMER: "This blender is a piece of *& %$!"

(This comment is repeated, increasingly louder, while Carlos deafs him.)

CUSTOMER: "Hey Buddy, I said, 'This blender is *& %$!' *Are you deaf or what?*" (*This* is the attack.)

CARLOS (stops tagging clearance items, smiles as if he is genuinely glad to see the irate customer): "Oh, hi, Sir. How can I help you?" (The attack is neutralized.)

Again, the customer can back off and be reasonable ("I bought this blender and it fell apart") or he can continue to holler and be abusive. However, by continuing to scream at friendly Carlos, the manipulator is going to look like a real jerk and accomplish nothing. Other people observing will probably start empathizing with Carlos.

Marcy only needed to employ Level Two twice on her mother (regarding the occasional baby-sitting request) to stop her mom's consistent response.

MOM: "That's the only time so far this year that your father and I had planned to go out . . . but we'll cancel our plans . . . Don't fret, we'll watch the kids."

MARCY: "Great, Mom, thanks. . . . See you at seven."

Simple and elegant.

Marcy refused to be baited, and her mother got little satisfaction. What is her mom going to say, "Hey, Marcy, if you don't buy into my guilt trips, I won't baby-sit?"

Why does Dave (who works for Attila the Hun) knock himself out trying to please his boss? And why is Dave's boss treating him that way? Why is Dave allowing it? Are guilt and fear involved here? You bet.

Continuing with our use of Level Two, Dave can respond to Attila the Hun like this.

ATTILA/BOSS: "Is that all you've gotten done?"

(Attila repeats this, increasingly louder, while Dave deafs him. Level One does not discourage Attila.)

BOSS: "I said, 'Is that all you've gotten done?' *Are you deaf or what?*"

DAVE (flashing a big smile): "Oh, hi, Boss. What can I do for you?"

Dave changed the rules and neutralized the manipulation. Dave gave the boss time to become reasonable. Starting all over again was openly irrational.

When we can experiment, when we can play, when we can treat ourselves lightly, we can explore the dimensions of communication. We can choose when and how to interact. We have that freedom. We do not have to be controlled and be manipulated.

Tess the Preteen finds Level Two useful. She seldom runs into more than a couple of annoying peers at a time, and even then she has a friend or two close by. She can afford to be gracious.

FELLOW STUDENT: "Hey, Tess, who cut your hair . . . your baby brother?"

(Tess deafs him several times as he repeats this. She continues talking to her friend, digging in her locker, looking at her book.)

FELLOW STUDENT: "Yo, Tess, I said, 'Who cut your hair, your baby brother?' Har, har."

(Tess moves on to Level Two.)

TESS (with a big smile): "Oh, Johnny, did you hear? Kathy's going out with Doug."

This is not the expected reaction. This is a non sequitur. The manipulative teen is confused and neutralized.

Nancy the Nurse has a hard time using Level Two with

her former patient. Even though she is not assigned to his room, she cannot withhold care or be rude. Of course, this is what the patient, who is playing "Now I gotcha," is hoping for. If she avoids the manipulation, but pays attention to the patient, she shoots herself in the foot. It is self-defeating since this is what he wants in the first place. She could ignore his calling her name for a while and then say, "Oh, hi, do you need me?" This just prolongs the agony. Next time, he'll yell "Nancy, help me" even louder.

Nancy could, of course, rush in to see him, completely covered with chocolate syrup from head and toe, and say, "Here I am, I was in the middle of taking care of one of *my* patients. Sorry I'm such a mess . . . bedpan duty, you know." However, this behavior (which is really not countering manipulation) is possible only if Nancy's supervisor is a drama major.

Fred, the Front Desk Manager, has already become involved in an unpleasant verbal exchange. ("Fred, how old are you?") Using Level One, Fred could have just walked away and pretended that he had suddenly gone deaf, although that is not at all appropriate, given his job. Level Two is even less appropriate. The employees and hotel guests will think Fred is out of touch if he suddenly says to the manipulator, "Oh, hi, what can I do for you?" after a verbal interaction with him. (On the other hand, given the strange behavior of some people in resort hotels, it just might fly.)

Level Two is also not appropriate for Clara, the closet apologizer, and Martin. Once a verbal exchange has occurred, it is difficult to deaf someone or to ignore the manipulation.

Catherine uses Levels One and Two repeatedly with Archie, her cousin. Most of the encounters, however, require a higher level to neutralize.

Once again, remember that the five levels of countering manipulation are increasingly potent. However, their *effectiveness* is not enhanced by using Level Five, for example, when Level One would have worked. By using Level One and Level Two, you can neutralize a significant number of manipulations. You can often ease the manipulator out of his or her subconscious need to control you. If repeated attempted manipulations fail to accomplish this goal (that is, transferring strength from you to the manipulator), the person trying to control you is likely to stop this behavior in your relationship.

ONCE MANIPULATION HAS BEEN NEUTRALIZED, THERE IS ROOM FOR THE RELATIONSHIP TO MEND.

Level Two is often the level of choice for those among us who have so-called bad habits. Let's say you buy and eat a whole sack of chocolate-covered donuts at one sitting—at home or in the office. Unless you are a closet donut eater, your donut eating is guaranteed to draw every manipulator in the vicinity, *instantly:*

"You shouldn't eat those things, they're fried in grease!"

"I sure wouldn't want to take a look at your cholesterol level after eating *those* things!"

"Don't you know how many calories you've just put in your body?"

Why are the manipulators doing this to you? Well, for one thing, are they jealous? Can their fear of eating donuts encourage them to try to make you feel fearful? Can their own guilt encourage them to try to make you feel guilty, too? Yep, to any or all three.

Basically, they perceive you as having more power than they do. How can you sit there like that, enjoying those terrible things, knowing how awful they are for your body? It's easy. You love eating these donuts; you are the one in charge of what goes in your mouth, and until donuts become illegal, you will do as you please. Thank you very much. And you'll probably do it again next week!

In essence, your eating those donuts makes a social statement. The things that are bad to eat so far outnumber what's left okay to eat (heck, even some veggies make their own carcinogens), that you will simply do what you feel like doing.

Levels One and Two are gentle and can be used on family, friends, and co-workers. By using Levels One and Two (deafing both the manipulation and the manipulator, or deafing the manipulation and being friendly to the manipulator), you have remained neutral. You have given the manipulator the opportunity to approach you in a nonmanipulative fashion. You have said nothing that can hurt the manipulator or your relationship. And you have given the manipulative attempt *none* of your energy.

How can someone slime you when you have not even heard what was said? In the last chapter, employing the principles of the martial arts, we compared Level One to walking away from the attacker. No contest. No fight. Here at Level Two, imagine two people. One is the attacker, and the other the intended victim—you. You need to be aware of your assailant. You know that the attack is a compliment. You stay alert, calm, and relaxed. A blow comes your way. Using circular motion instead of straight, you move out of the way so that the blow goes right on by you. Acting as if nothing happened, which is true, you then greet your opponent with a cheerful comment like "Pretty day today."

Words carry an enormous power. So does silence.

You may possibly have a concern at this point, that is that Levels One and Two are wishy-washy. They are not. There is a difference between the martial arts philosophy and the ol' Western shoot-em-out-in-the-street way of doing things. And it is *precisely* this difference that gives you the edge. In order to fully understand this, you need to put yourself into your opponent's shoes and into any spectator's mind.

Ask yourself: Who has the greater power and strength? Who commands the greater respect? The person who falls apart and gets into an argument that most likely will be lost? Or the person who simply won't be baited, who views this verbal attack as unimportant? And continues life's journey *uninterrupted* by this *distraction?*

Ask yourself: Am I underestimating what any witnesses are observing? Could they be getting the old slimy feeling also? Do they honestly think I am weak for deafing this behavior? No. Definitely not.

Finally, ask yourself from the viewpoint of the *manipulator:* What is worse than being counterattacked? Could it be *being ignored?* Your manipulative behavior is so ridiculous that it doesn't even warrant a reply. Your verbal behavior is not worth the time of day. A counterattack from your victim at least validates you. Being deafed not only *invalidates* your manipulative behavior, but it makes you doubt yourself in the process.

HOW CAN YOU, THE MANIPULATOR, GLOAT . . . WHEN YOU HAVEN'T EVEN GOTTEN SOMEBODY'S GOAT?

Let's go back to the viewpoint of the one being manipulated. When you start using Levels One and Two, and consciously incorporating them into your lifestyle, you will notice a dramatic difference in your attitude and in the attitude of the manipulators toward you. You will recognize the manipulators, and neutralize their manipulations. You will observe an increase in respect from these people. You do not have to dazzle a manipulator and any witnesses with a Level Five classic comeback in order to achieve your goal of stopping the manipulations. You will actually see a change in behavior by many former manipulators when you employ Levels One and Two. They will respect you (they are unable to get any of your power), and they will stop their offensive behavior. Or they will become more desperate (because now *you* have *their* goat), and you can counter the manipulations at a higher level until the behavior stops.

You, the reader, can begin at any time using these techniques. Ask yourself where you might use Level One and Level Two at work, at home, in the day-to-day encounters of your life. Just identifying manipulations in your own life is a start. Just employing the soft martial arts principles lets you be the one in control of the manipulations that you will encounter. You are viewed as the one having the greater strength anyway. Now you have the opportunity to prove it. No longer the manipulated, no longer the victim.

By the way, the motto for Level Two is "Have a nice day, anyway."

To summarize Level Two:

1. Take the manipulative attempt as a compliment.
2. Know that you have the upper hand—the greater power in the relationship at this point.
3. Be kind to friends, family, and co-workers who are trying to manipulate you, yet totally ignore their manipulative behavior.
4. Resist the urge to counterattack.

CHAPTER 6

Permission:
Level Three

What if there has been a genuine lack of communication, and we assume manipulative intentions by someone who is quite simply not focusing on us in that way? Sometimes we are all too ready to take on someone else's problem as our own. Or, we are so caught up in our own agenda that we don't take the extra minute or two to clarify the circumstances.

Here's the scenario: You are out of shape physically. You've slept all winter. You were counting on joining the office volleyball team. However, you totaled your back helping a friend move last week. Everyone knows that you are now under a doctor's care and can't play. You hear about how *tough* the first volleyball practice was. Your best friend complains to you. Trying to show interest, you approach another friend on the team and say, "Hear it was really rough the first day of practice."

Your friend replies, "I enjoyed it. . . . It isn't rough if you're in shape."

You immediately get defensive. He is insinuating that *you* are not in shape—you who need to work out, lose a few pounds, whatever.

Have you ever considered that he may really have meant something entirely different? It is a possibility that

1. He means that because your back hurts, you're in no shape to play volleyball.
2. He is implying that they (the rest of the team who bitched and moaned) are not in shape and that's why it is hard for them.
3. Calling you a couch potato hasn't even occurred to him.

Something is said that can be taken one of two different ways. When our defenses are on overload for any number of reasons, we sometimes automatically assume the worst.

A true example illustrates one common problem in communication: The husband gets awakened at 4:00 A.M. on Valentine's Day by the blaring of the car horn, which is stuck. Flashlight in hand, freezing in his pajamas, he accidentally rips out the headlight cables along with the horn wires. While up, he notices the outside hose and faucet are frozen solid since the temperature is only twelve degrees. Coming inside, he trips over a tricycle and twists his ankle. He hobbles off to work at 6 A.M., pleased that his wife and two small children are still fast asleep. He has planned a special surprise for his wife that evening. On the way home from work, he'll pick up a dozen long-stemmed red roses and also a six-week-old kitten, something she's always wanted. He left this note for her in the meantime:

"Honey, please take the car down to the mechanic. I ripped out the headlight cables. Please call the plumber to fix the frozen pipes. Happy Valentine's Day. I love you."

When she gets up, she reads the note and feels awful. Other people at least get candy on Valentine's Day.

Now, can you imagine what a joy she may be today

while interacting with her environment? Will she be Mary Poppins taking the car down? Will she be jovial to the plumber?

Later, when the plumber wishes her Happy Valentine's Day, he'll receive a sarcastic comment for his trouble. Just as the auto mechanic will. Now both the plumber and the auto mechanic are bummed out. See how it works? They may even decide to forget doing something nice for their special people. Poor communication truly creates a domino effect in our lives and other people's lives.

So, in Level Three we will find out whether an encounter is truly a manipulation directed at us or not. We will give the perceived *manipulator a chance to come clean.*

If the perceived manipulator did not consciously or subconsciously intend to control or hurt the intended victim, he or she will usually back off immediately when confronted with the manipulation.

In the Valentine example above, the auto mechanic replies, "I feel awful. . . . What did I say?"

If the wife responds, "I'm sorry I hollered at you. I think my husband hates me," he can feel compassion for her and go on with the rest of his day.

If she replies, "You men are all the same," he knows that he is in a manipulative situation. Period.

If you discover that you are in a truly manipulative situation, not a lack of communication, then you give permission to the manipulator to manipulate, but you will not be a party to it.

You give the manipulators the opportunity to be themselves, whatever that may be. If they want to feel and act like manipulators, that is their choice, but you are not going to be involved.

> THE MANIPULATOR IS GIVEN *PERMISSION*
> TO BEHAVE AS A MANIPULATOR, BUT YOU,
> THE INTENDED VICTIM, ARE NOT GOING
> TO BE INVOLVED IN THIS MANIPULATION
> IN ANY WAY.

When you confront the manipulator, by becoming vulnerable yourself, you allow for correction of the behavior toward you. Keeping this in mind, let's look at the following tale about a little boy and his whistle. This true incident was resolved at Level Three.

> You are camping at a popular campground right by the river. Quiet hours are from 10:00 P.M. To 7:00 A.M. At 7:01 A.M., you are catapulted into consciousness by a little boy tricycling by, blowing a police whistle. The child continues to entertain the campground for the next twelve hours. The father looks like a Sumo wrestler. Both parents are encouraging the child. Your son attempts to borrow the whistle, even buy the whistle, but to no avail. The kid loves that whistle; his mom gave it to him that very morning as a special surprise. Solutions from other distraught campers include buying a bugle for your son to blow reveille at 2:00 A.M. outside *their* tent; snatching the kid, hauling him five miles up the river, and telling him to walk back *slowly;* and packing up the tent and leaving.

We are not suggesting that this little boy is a manipulator, even though he may be enjoying the attention. His parents may only have a case of insensitivity. Yet, we can ask ourselves the following questions. Has this child managed to change how the campers feel? Yes, they are feeling somewhat stressed right now. Has this child managed to change how the campers think? Yes, law-abiding citizens are now contemplating doing the unthinkable to this kid. Has this child managed to change how the campers behave? Yes, some campers may pack up and leave.

An older camper yells over to the child, who is standing by his mother: "Love that whistle, kid. . . . Can't you blow it any *louder?*"

"Whadda he say?" asks the kid.

The mother responds, "That nice man said he *loves* your whistle, Bobbie, he wants you to blow it *louder.*" (Honest to God, this happened in real life.)

The camper was last seen asking directions from the park ranger for the way to the nearest tavern.

This type of example lends itself readily to a Level Three, especially since it is not a one-on-one manipulation. In fact, you don't know whether manipulation actually exists. This whistler has not assaulted you personally, even though he has done in the whole campground.

You are between a rock and a hard spot: Go to Whistler's Mother or go to Sumo Dad? Well, Mom gave the child the whistle. Dad didn't. Maybe Dad is getting tired of it by now.

The campers draw up an informal lottery. You win. You go to the dad and say, "Pardon me, I understand your child needs to play, but my nerves are shot and that whistle isn't helping. Besides, I'm not looking forward to going to bed tonight, knowing how I'll wake up at seven A.M."

Believe it or not, Level Three works. Dad simply says, "Hey, I'll disappear the whistle."

Five words to paradise.

So, at Level Three, you are past the stages of deafing and deafing/disarming. You are confronting (not attacking) and simply and vulnerably telling the perceived manipulator how you feel. We suggest that you use the first-person pronoun (I), rather than the second-person pronoun (you). You can experience the difference using the camping example, above.

Using the first-person pronoun:

"Pardon me, *I* understand your child needs to play, but *my* nerves are shot and that whistle isn't helping. Besides *I'm* not looking forward . . . seven A.M."

A response using the second-person pronoun might be the following:

"Why are *you* allowing *your* child to disturb the whole campground with that whistle?"

Can you see how the first comment allows more freedom for an open exchange of ideas and a possible solution?

Using the second-person viewpoint ("Why are *you* . . .") can put the listener on the defensive. Sumo Dad may just decide to defend to the death the right of his son to blow that whistle.

Let's say you become vulnerable and express your feelings. Instead of resolving the conflict, the manipulators deny the manipulative behavior, or respond with "I don't give a———how you feel," or try to provoke an argument. Then you can be almost certain that you are dealing with manipulation. You then can make it perfectly clear that the manipulators can continue to be themselves, but you won't be a party to it. (In the camping example you will "put in your earplugs.")

The key message here is "*I understand; I will not participate; I have other things I prefer to do now.*" You stand your ground. There is no room for further argument. You will not be baited. You have other things that you prefer to do that are more important than being involved in this manipulation attempt.

Let's see how Marcy and her mom, Martin the club member, and Nancy the nurse use Level Three's techniques.

MARCY AND HER MOM

MOM: "Marcy, you know I'd love to watch the kids for you next Saturday, but that was the one evening that your father and I had planned to stay home and be together . . . but never mind, that's okay, we'll be happy to cancel our plans and do it."

MARCY: "Mom, I feel guilty when I ask you to baby-sit."

MOM (honest response): "Guilty?"

MARCY: "You always have to cancel or change your plans and it makes me feel guilty."

MOM: "I didn't mean to make you feel guilty. I guess I just didn't want you to know I'm really hanging around here waiting for you to ask me to help. I'm sorry."

Or:

MOM (manipulative response): "What do you mean, feel guilty? I already told you I'd baby-sit for you on Saturday!"

Then Marcy responds something like this:

MARCY: "Fine, Mom, I understand the way you feel. I need to take the cookies out of the oven now. See you on Saturday."

And she gets off the phone.

MARTIN THE CLUB MEMBER

CLARA: "That wasn't me you saw downtown, Martin."

MARTIN: "I feel really foolish when you say you weren't there."

CLARA (honest response): "I guess I'm just bitchy lately. I'm sorry; that was me downtown."

Or:

CLARA (manipulative response): "I told you I wasn't downtown this morning. Do you want to make a federal case out of it?"

The first response won't happen too often, but it could. More likely, Martin will get the second. He then responds:

MARTIN: "Well, Clara, if you want to feel that way, you can. I'm not going to argue." The "I understand, but . . ." is implied here.

Martin gives it no emotion. He is not mad, not upset. Clara has his permission to behave any way that she feels like behaving. He simply will not get involved in it. He has taken evasive action, and Clara can continue, now or in the future, to play this game out, but without Martin.

NANCY THE NURSE

PESKY PATIENT (ring, ring): "Hey, Nancy, come in here, I want a glass of juice. . . . My IV is running backward. . . . I need help reaching the phone." (The family is sitting around.)

NANCY: "You know, I feel so guilty when you want my help."

PESKY PATIENT (honest response): "Well, I feel I'm entitled to the best care there is. And you are one great nurse. I guess I'm out of bounds, though, knowing it could get you in trouble. I'm sorry. You need to take care of your other patients."

This *could* happen. When reasonable people realize that they are making unreasonable demands, they sometimes fess up. Can you remember a time when you expected too much from someone and confessed that to them?

On the other hand, the response may well be like the following:

PESKY PATIENT (manipulative response): "You feel guilty? I'm the patient and I'm entitled to decent care. I'm lying here recovering from surgery and you feel guilty?"

Nancy then can respond with the following:

NANCY: "It is your right to request good service." (She leaves.)

Or Nancy could say, "I understand," as she leaves the room.

Now let's explore what we are trying to do here in terms of the martial arts principles.

Let's say you are standing in the middle of the room. An attacker charges you. You take evasive action. You move in a circular motion. You pivot and do a ninety-degree side-step. The attacker misses you and crashes into the wall. You always keep your eyes on your attacker. You are relaxed but alert. You have no emotion about this at all.

If it has been an honest mistake, and the other person only tripped over the doorjamb and fell toward you, you will get an apology. "Gosh, I almost ran into you. Sorry, I tripped." If the perceived attacker is a manipulator, you will see more.

At this point you make it clear to the attacker that he or she can keep this up all day and continue to charge at you, but you will take evasive action each time. Both you and the wall behind you simply don't care.

Level Three is a bit more complex than Level One and Level Two because of its philosophies and principles. After all, most of us have been exposed to Levels One and Two in some fashion over the years, although they haven't been defined as such. Your mother may have told you to ignore the school bully. A friend may have told you to turn the other cheek. So let's summarize Level Three and look at any concerns you may have at this point.

In an attempt to discover whether true manipulation is taking place or not, you simply and vulnerably tell the perceived manipulators how you feel. For example:

"I feel guilty whenever I ask a favor of you."

"It makes me angry when I'm teased."

"I feel embarrassed when I look like a fool."

"I'm afraid I don't understand what I just heard." (Generic version.)

You have now allowed the perceived manipulator the opportunity to continue communication, to apologize, or to give a reasonable explanation that removes the encounter from the manipulation category.

If the person takes this opportunity, the rewards are obvious: You have not become a victim. You have not contributed to a broken relationship. You have not made a fool out of yourself by going for the other person's throat when it was a simple communication disaster.

If, on the other hand, you receive an argument or a denial after telling the person how you feel, you can be almost certain that you are being manipulated. Now, we recognize at this point that you have every reason for wanting blood. Until you have incorporated these noncombative principles into your "very soul" (that is, used them a few times with success), you may be feeling somewhat angry or guilty from the initial manipulative attempt. You may also be feeling the additional disappointment of realizing that this other person is going to keep on trying to manipulate you unless you do something about it.

Now it is very important for you *not* to counterattack. Remember that you made yourself vulnerable when confronting Sumo Dad. It was important that you did not counterattack, for example, by saying, "The next time I hear that whistle, you can expect to wake up to a bugle playing reveille outside your tent."

FORGIVENESS

> THE GOLDEN RULE IN COUNTERING MANIPULATORS IS TO FORGIVE

Forgiveness fits in because it is actually the first step in countering manipulation. Commit this to memory. It is important. Forgiveness is actually the first step in countering manipulation. It is not one of the five techniques. However, it makes using the techniques easier.

When it appears that someone is trying to shoot you down, it does give you a significant advantage to realize that he or she is envious of you, and views you as more important.

Forgiveness means that you are big enough to open your heart to someone and say, either out loud or inside you, "I can extend compassion. . . ." With forgiveness, you release the anger and hurt and let go. If you can approach a lifelong history of manipulation, or a single encounter, with forgiveness first, the five levels of countering manipulation will be far more effective than if you come from a point of feeling like a victim. Or seeking revenge. The threat is just not the same when you realize that it comes at you from a point of envy, weakness, and powerlessness.

•••

Back to our characters. This is how Dave who works for Attila the Hun, Annie the Airhead, and Tess the preteen could neutralize their manipulators using Level Three:

DAVE WHO WORKS FOR ATTILA THE HUN

ATTILA/BOSS (handing Dave a whole week's worth of work): "I want this done by noon."

DAVE (enthusiastically): "Okey-dokey, no problem, I'll have it done by noon. Happy to do it. Noon, you say?"

(Noon comes . . . da da Da DA!)

ATTILA/BOSS: "I thought you said you'd get this done by noon. You're not finished."

DAVE: "I'm working as fast as I can." (Shows vulnerability.)

ATTILA/BOSS (honest response): "I guess there is a limit to how much can be physically accomplished."

This is pretty lame, we admit, but anything is possible, and he may back off if he stops to think about it.

Or:

ATTILA/BOSS (manipulative response): "I expected you to get this work done by noon. And it isn't done."

DAVE: "I understand how you feel, but I can only do my best."

If Attila continues to harangue him, Dave needs to use Level Two until he can get physically away (men's room, coffee break, etc.) to consider how and when to use Level Four or Five. At this point, he may also want to ask himself how much this job really means to him.

ANNIE THE AIRHEAD

CO-WORKER: "Hey, Annie, how many Annies does it take to change a light bulb?"

ANNIE: "I feel hurt when you guys tease me all the time."

Her co-workers are likely to respond one of two ways.

CO-WORKER (honest response): "Gosh, Annie, we think you're cute. We were just trying to give you a bad time. I mean, we like you, that's why we tease you; we didn't mean to hurt you. We're sorry."

Or:

CO-WORKER (manipulative response): *"Tease you? . . . What do you mean, 'tease you'? You got a chip on your shoulder or what?"*

The co-worker's honest response may very well end the manipulation now, as well as prevent future encounters. Annie's Level Three then has achieved its purpose. However, if a variation on the second response occurs, Annie remains in a manipulative environment. Then she makes it clear that she had no further desire to be a party to the manipulations:

ANNIE: "I understand how you feel, but I'm not participating."

Annie then continues to use Levels One or Two (deafing and deafing/disarming), unless she chooses to go on to Level Four or Five. She does not get drawn into further discussion about the teasing.

TESS THE PRETEEN

FELLOW STUDENT (at soccer practice): "Hey, Tess, if you tried harder, the ball might move, ha, ha."

TESS: "I feel like a klutz."

FELLOW STUDENT (honest response): "I didn't mean for it to come out that way. I'm sorry."

Or:

FELLOW STUDENT (manipulative response): "Well,

you are a klutz. I'm just being honest with you.''

TESS: ''Whatever turns you on.''

And Tess turns her attention elsewhere. The ''I understand, but . . .'' is inherent in her response. Again, from now on, unless Tess decides to go to Level Four or Five, she'll attempt to deaf her fellow student.

Remember that most manipulations are done on a subconscious level. Often the person manipulating doesn't even recognize that he or she is doing it. You cannot get into a logical discussion about something that both of you can't even define. Argument will simply lead to even further argument.

> The manipulators will try to make everything your responsibility.
>
> The manipulators will try to convince you that you are crazy.
>
> The manipulators will try to make you feel even greater fear or guilt.

The manipulators gain their greatest power from you when your negative reactions escalate and you respond with a counterattack. Remember the importance of remaining calm and giving none of your energy back to the manipulator? Remember in the last chapter when we asked, How can those manipulators gloat, when they haven't even gotten your goat?

It is important that they do not get your goat. You want to take evasive action so that the manipulators' negative energy does not slime you, but returns to them, and their own goat gets gotten! And then they will stop trying to manipulate you. Because they will realize they cannot have any of your strength and power. They end up stuck with their own negative energy and this does not feel good. You will be pleasantly surprised the first time you successfully neutralize a manipulation instead of counterattacking. You'll receive a power jolt that significantly raises your self-esteem!

Sexy Sheila and Carlos in Customer Service have learned how to use Level Three to deflect the manipulators. This is what they do:

SEXY SHEILA

MALE CO-WORKER (RANDY) (in front of several employees): "Hey, Sam, I won the lotto. I get to spend the afternoon making it with Sheila in the boardroom."

SHEILA: "You know, I feel embarrassed when men tease me."

MALE CO-WORKER (RANDY) (honest response): "Hey, Sheila, I'm just kidding. I thought you wanted to be treated like one of the guys. Hey, if it bothers you, I won't do it anymore. I didn't mean to harass you."

Or:

MALE CO-WORKER (RANDY) (manipulative response): "Hey, baby, I'm just paying you a compliment. ... Why, little ol' Randy here is just kidding. ... Can't take the heat, huh?"

SHEILA: "You can feel any way you like Randy, I'm not participating."

Sheila has given Randy the opportunity to correct his behavior. He has chosen not to accept. She lets him know that he can feel whatever he wants to feel, but she is not going to get involved.

CARLOS THE CUSTOMER SERVICE
REPRESENTATIVE

CUSTOMER: "This blender is a piece of *& %$#. I'll have you know I'm no sucker, you'll pay for this. . . ."

CARLOS: "I sure get uptight in this job when people yell at me."

CUSTOMER (honest response): "I'm sorry, you know. . . . Maybe I feel like punching someone's face in today. Listen, would you believe . . . I lost my job, wrecked my car, my girlfriend left me, and I had a UFO experience, all in the past three days. Like, man, I feel totally out of control."

This response sounds bizarre, but you would be surprised at the way many people (especially strangers) will react to your vulnerability, especially if their whole life is turned upside down. You may or may not wish to comfort this person (although you'll get stars in your heavenly crown if you do). At the very least, you'll know that what appeared to be a direct frontal attack on you had nothing to do with you at all.

The following experience happened to the one of the authors.

A friend and I went out to a fancy restaurant to celebrate my birthday. Dinner was expensive there, about a week's wages by my standards. (We were both poor college students.) I ordered steak. My dinner arrived, and it was completely burned. It was like trying to eat a charcoal briquette.

My friend called the waiter over. The waiter got all huffy and tried to minimize the problem. I excused myself. I walked into the kitchen and asked for the chef. I went up to him and asked him "What happened to my dinner?"

Tears welled up in his eyes. He asked me if he could join our table. I said sure.

The chef sat with us. Tall white hat and all. He told us that his son had been arrested that day, and his wife had freaked out and had left him. He was in agony. We listened and tried our best to help and counsel him.

The restaurant gave us complimentary rain checks, but that seemed the least of our worries.

Back to Carlos dealing with the abusive customer and the broken blender. Let's say Carlos doesn't end up playing psychotherapist to this man.

CARLOS: "I sure get uptight in this job when people yell at me."

CUSTOMER (manipulative response): "Yell at you? This blender is a—"

CARLOS: "You're right. Here, fill out these forms."

CUSTOMER: "I'll have your job for this."

CARLOS: "I understand. Please add it on the bottom of the form."

Carlos simply gives no energy to arguing with this man. He has given the man the opportunity to act responsibly. The man has not chosen to take it. If Carlos used Levels One and Two, he has given the man three opportunities by now. It is the customer's problem.

• • •

The positive payoff for you if you choose to follow Level Three's advice to neutralize and not counterattack will be threefold:

(1) You have made it clear that you are not going to keep this negative energy. You have gained your freedom and kept your integrity. You have made it clear that you are not a victim.

(2) You have said and done nothing to damage the relationship. You have not escalated the power struggle. You have no guilt that you may have indeed hurt the manipulator in a big way by counterattacking. No hollow victory. You have cut no tapes to play over and over again in your mind. "Well, I sure told him off, I did. I made him look like a total fool!" Playing the tapes of the argument over and over again takes a lot of your own personal energy. It does.

(3) By not counterattacking and not hurting the other person (whether deserved or not), by refusing to keep the negative energy, you have established your own personal power base. This is genuine power that does not come from feeding off other people's power. It is a genuine power that lives within you. You, not the manipulators, are in control of you.

But, you ask, aren't the manipulators going to think I'm a total geek for not fighting back? No. If you fight back, you're using their rules. If you take evasive action and then neutralize the manipulation, you're using your own rules. You have made it perfectly clear that their manipulative behavior is not even worthy of your further time or comment. You simply have more important things to do. *Remember, they viewed you as more powerful than themselves to start with, or they wouldn't have tried to manipulate you in the first place.* So you will simply reinforce this. You are more powerful than they are. Powerful people are busy

living life. You are too busy to continue this crazy manipulation business.

Again, the key phrase to remember here is "I understand,
but . . . [I will not participate, I have other things I prefer
to do now.]" And hold your ground. This implies compassion. The manipulators have the right to be manipulators,
but without you, thank you.

Although Level Three is not the level of choice for Fred
the front desk manager or for Catherine and her cousin,
let's see what happens when they decide to use Level
Three.

FRED THE FRONT DESK MANAGER

HOTEL GUEST: "Hey, Fred, how old are you?"

FRED: "Forty-seven."

HOTEL GUEST: "I never knew a guy named Fred to
live past the age of fifty."

FRED: "I'm afraid I don't understand what I just
heard."

HOTEL GUEST (honest response, though there probably
isn't one): "I was just trying to be funny. Sorry."

Or:

HOTEL GUEST (manipulative response): "Whadda ya
mean, you don't understand? I only said . . . Oh, big deal!"

Fred responds with the following:

FRED: "I understand, but I have other things that I need
to attend to now."

Can you see here how Fred is refusing to give any energy
to the manipulation? Can you see here how Fred is giving
the hotel guest permission to be himself, to work his manipulation, but work it *alone?* Fred is not arguing. Fred is
not counterattacking. Fred confronts the manipulative be-

havior. And Fred makes it clear that he will not be a party to this behavior.

However, Fred still wants to employ a higher level.

CATHERINE AND HER COUSIN

ARCHIE: "Those sons of————in Congress better not raise my taxes! Stupid idiots! Handing out money for welfare and unwed mothers! Bleeding hearts all of them! Pollution control, military expenditures . . . just a bunch of hypocrites!

CATHERINE: "I feel really vulnerable when I hear you go on and on like this. It upsets me, too."

ARCHIE (honest response): "I'm scared. I have no control over whether I live or die, much less what goes on in the rest of the world. I'm sorry I'm upsetting you, Catherine."

This is an unlikely response.

More likely, something like the following will occur:

ARCHIE (manipulative response): "I'm one opinionated old geezer, I am. And proud of it. This country is based on the likes of me."

CATHERINE: "You can feel however you wish, Archie. I'm going to go take a nap now."

The situation is thus diffused. What Catherine needs to do here is to convince Archie that he needs counseling. She is in no position to act as his psychotherapist.

Another thing to keep in mind is to be cautious using Level Three in particularly nasty manipulations. Becoming vulnerable and telling a lifelong master of manipulation how you feel in an *obvious* manipulation defeats the purpose of Level Three—which is to determine whether manipulation exists in the first place. If you use Level Three for obvious manipulations, all you've done, then, is become vulnerable. You probably will not change the manipulator's behavior. And you may have set yourself up for more manipulation.

The motto for Level Three Counter-Manipulation (when you have determined that manipulation does exist) is "A Thorn By Any Other Name Is Still a Thorn."

The essential techniques of Level Three are the following:

1. You try to determine whether manipulation truly exists.
2. Using the first person ("I" statements), you tell the perceived manipulator how you feel.
3. By becoming vulnerable, you allow open communication and a resolution of the conflict.
4. If this does not occur and the person continues to manipulate, you respond with empathy (I understand, but . . .).
5. You show that you will not be involved with this. The manipulator can continue manipulating, but he or she will be doing it alone.
6. You do *not* counterattack; you do not let yourself get baited into an argument. You play by using your rules: evasive action followed by neutralization.

Can you see how using Level Three might have helped our lady in the Valentine story at the beginning of this chapter? If you recall, our Valentine lady felt terrible: Everybody else gets something special from her sweetheart. She received a note asking her to take the car to the mechanic and to call the plumber about the frozen pipes. She doesn't know that her husband was up in the wee hours handling problems. She doesn't know that he plans to surprise her with roses and a kitten that evening.

Had she phoned her husband at work and told him how

she felt ("I'm feeling crummy, isn't there more to Valentine's Day than this?") he would have reassured her that he was not trying to manipulate her. It was simply a communication failure.

Can you see where some people might use Level Three before using Levels One and Two? Some people who are blessed with outstanding communication skills (or feel compelled to straighten things out immediately) might want to employ Level Three right from the beginning, and then move on to Levels One and Two if manipulation appears to exist.

As you become familiar with the levels and the ease of accelerating or dropping down in intensity among these levels, you may wish to experiment using Level Three right from the start, knowing that you can go straight to Level Four or Five if you choose.

Now that we have explored Level Three, let's take a look at Level Four.

CHAPTER 7

Focused Attention:
Level Four

Now you're going to start getting tough. The focused attention of Level Four and the reversal of Level Five are reserved for the more intractable manipulative attempts. These levels, as did the others, follow the soft martial arts principles. They represent the neutralization techniques that are used when the aggressor steps up the level of attack and continues to press his or her perceived advantage.

In Level Four, you pay attention to the manipulator in an exaggerated manner. To illustrate this exaggeration, the motto of this technique is "Please wait while you embarrass yourself with your own words." The authors use a couple of standard scripts, which we will share with you.

The essential core of Level Four is to hold up the manipulator's behavior for someone else to see and observe. The witnesses you select can be real or imaginary. By using Level Four, you're conveying the following: "I know what you're trying to pull off, even if you don't; and I want you to know it is now public knowledge." In Level Four, there is no room for argument following use of this countering technique. After you have finished using Level Four, you'll

change the subject, or get off the phone, or temporarily
leave the vicinity.

The following incident illustrates Level Four in action.

Imagine you are the coach for your kid's soccer team.
In this one particular game, the coach of the opposing
team seems to be out for blood. He is abusive to the
refs and even to the kids.

Throughout the game, he is doing things that are tech-
nically acceptable but against the spirit of the game.
He is holding kids back on the bench without letting
them play, or provoking them into unnecessarily
rough behavior. No one on his team seems to be enjoying the game except him.

Near the end of the game your team, too, is depressed
and losing. You call a time-out and go over to have
a chat with this person. You don't get any further
than "Hey. The team and I are feeling crumm—"
when he responds with "I don't give a damn how
you feel. I'll play the game any way I see fit!"

Before you decide on violence as a solution, give a version of Level Four a try. First, forgive him for his obnoxious behavior, accept the compliment that he thinks you are
so good that he has to insult you, and do the following
Level Four:

Loud enough to be heard, and in front of a couple of
parents standing nearby, respond with "You know, the
guys from my team and I had a little bet going. Personally,
I said that you'd never do this sort of thing anymore, but
everyone else said you couldn't help yourself. Anyway,
I've got to go and pay off the others." Then leave.

That's it. It does not matter if he checks your story. The

negative energy has been neutralized, and the manipulator will think twice before doing that again with you around.

Using Level Four involves a script to focus attention on the manipulator. Two such scripts are presented here for your use. They are easy to use, adaptable to many situations, and require no memorization.

In the first version you call someone else over (a friend or acquaintance, or even an innocent bystander). Then you ask the manipulator to repeat *exactly* what he or she just said—in front of this new person. The second version uses a bet, as in the soccer coach example above. You tell the manipulator that you had a bet that he or she wouldn't do this anymore. You lost, and now you have to *leave* to pay off the bet. There must be no room for argument. Alternatively, you can use the phone in order to reach a *third* person who is going to be so pleased that they won the bet. You act as if you're on the side of the manipulator. You had bet your friend, mother, or someone else, that the manipulator wouldn't pull this stuff anymore. Your friend or mother, or someone else, bet that the manipulator would. It's that simple. Deliberately remain vague about naming the manipulation, if you can. And don't call it a manipulation. If you do, you'll possibly get derailed into an argument.

Essentially, in Level Four, you focus attention on the manipulator in a big way. You can make up other scripts that work just as well or better. In short, in cases of obvious verbal insults or manipulation, you are drawing attention to the manipulator. You are powerful enough to hold the manipulator publicly accountable for his or her unacceptable behavior.

At this point, you may be wondering if we are asking you to lie in the "bet" version of Level Four. If it makes you feel more comfortable, then make a verbal bet (no money involved) with a close friend. Bet your friend that all the manipulators in your life will stop trying to manipulate you. Have your friend bet that they won't stop.

Now let's run Level Four past our characters from the previous chapter. Annie the Airhead used the second script with a telephone call.

ANNIE THE AIRHEAD

CO-WORKER: "Hey, Annie, how many Annies does it take to change a light bulb?"

ANNIE: "I can't believe this. I have a twenty-dollar bet with Helen that you guys had stopped this. She bet me you'd keep it up. I gotta call her. Boy, is she gonna be happy. What . . . ? Never mind. This is too much!" (Dialing the weather number, Annie pretends to call Helen.) "Hey, Helen, you aren't going to believe this. . . ."

Do not let the manipulator get a word in edgewise. Period. You are the good guy—you have bet that the manipulator wouldn't pull this stuff again. Another person bet that the manipulator would. Now you need to let this other person know that he or she has won the bet. Our characters from before will show you how to carry out Level Four in various circumstances.

There are several ways that you can improvise on this technique. Using it requires that another person be witnessing or be aware of the manipulator in action. Another person, or persons (real or fictitious), are there with you, in person or in thought, observing the unacceptable behavior. *You are not daring the manipulator by accusing him or her of the attempt. You are merely coming from such a point of power that you can hold up the manipulative behavior for other people to recognize.* You hold it up for scrutiny.

But be careful not to call it a manipulative attempt, in order to prevent argument by the manipulator.

MARCY AND HER MOM

Because Marcy was already on the telephone with her mom, she used a different variation of the script. Her husband, with whom she had made the bet, appeared in the room while she was talking on the telephone to her mom:

MOM: "That's just fine, we'll cancel our plans and be happy to baby-sit for you on Saturday."

MARCY: "I can't believe you just said that, Mom. I have a twenty-dollar bet with Joe that you had given up this sort of thing, that you'd never do it again. He swore you would. Oh, here's Joe, now. Gotta run, see you on Saturday." And Marcy gets off the phone fast. She leaves no room for an argument. When her mom calls back, she shrugs off any references as unimportant unless her mom does it again.

TESS THE PRETEEN

Tess found it convenient to use the first version of the script. There were already several of her friends on the school playground.

FELLOW STUDENT: "Who buys your clothes, Tess, the school principal?"

TESS: "Hey, Anna, Chris, come over here and get a load of this. I can't believe it. . . . Tell Anna and Chris exactly what you just asked me."

This is attracting much attention to the manipulator. Many young manipulators don't like to chance this type of hype.

FRED THE FRONT DESK MANAGER

Fred used another variation of the first version. Many people were already present in the hotel lobby, and several of them had heard the initial encounter.

HOTEL GUEST: "I never knew a guy named Fred to live past the age of fifty."

FRED (in a loud voice, so that those who were in the lobby could easily hear): "You're too much. I have a bet riding with my boss that I could get through this entire shift without having to deal with a smart aleck. He said no. I'd be sure to have someone. Excuse me. I've gotta go pay him off."

DAVE WHO WORKS FOR THE ATTILA THE HUN

Dave's script is similar to Fred's, because several fellow office workers are already present.

ATTILA/BOSS: "Is that all you have done? You told me that you'd have everything done by noon."

DAVE: "Hells, bells, I lost again. I had a bet with Frank [the first name of the personnel director helps, whether Dave knows him or not] that you wouldn't do this to me anymore. He bet me that you'd keep doing it. I swore that you'd stopped. Now I owe him a fishing trip. I'll be back in a couple of minutes."

Dave leaves and leaves fast. He doesn't allow any room for argument. In order for Level Four to work, there can be no room for discussion.

MARTIN THE CLUB MEMBER

Martin uses a slightly different variation on the telephone call script, without actually picking up the phone.

CLARA: "That wasn't me you saw downtown, Martin."

MARTIN: "This is too much. I bet Ted [mutual friend] that you were over this kick and he bet me that you weren't. I've just got to call him and tell him he won. I'll see if he's home now." And Martin disappears to the men's room. No hesitation. No argument. Period. When he returns, the meeting is back in progress and the subject doesn't get brought up again.

Can you, as a reader, experience the pattern? It is simple: It is important that someone else (real or imaginary) is observing or being made aware of the manipulative person in action. You can do it with a four- or five-line script. You can invent your own scripts. And have them handy, to be used automatically when you need a Level Four.

Are you beginning to get a feel for the various levels? Can you grasp the progressively increasing potency involved in the use of Levels One through Four? Can you see where couples with successful, committed, and open relationships may already be using some of these same techniques, learned by trial and error? Have you ever observed a person in a powerful position who seems to navigate smoothly through a sea of manipulators and intimidators? He or she is probably using some of these same techniques, based on the same underlying principles. The principles that underlie the success of the martial arts also can be used to your advantage when dealing with a verbal assailant.

Can you look around and find some relationships in your life, where some versions of Levels One, Two, Three, and Four are being executed? What about all the men out there who deaf the manipulations of their wives or girlfriends (using Level Two), while inwardly saying to themselves, "It's *only* hormones, it's *only* hormones, it's *only.* . . . "

They choose not to counterattack, even when their partner snaps at them. What about the people whom you have seen take the extra time and effort to vulnerably explain how they feel (guilty, hurt, etc.) and whom are reassured to learn they are not being manipulated after all (Level Three)?

Can you appreciate that Level Four may share a bit in common with the initial stages of arbitration or mediation, where an outside party assists in settling a dispute? In an attempt to raise the consciousness level of a manipulator, Level Four requires you to let that person know that he or she is being observed by an outside party. The behavior is not going unnoticed. Maybe that's one reason that there are so many success stories about couples going through counseling together. In such counseling, the counselor plays the role of the outside observer. The couple receives support as each person becomes increasingly aware of the manipulation that may exist in the relationship. Then they try to understand how to go about correcting it. As the amount of manipulation decreases, communication increases and the relationship can mend.

Now, let's see how our last four characters use Level Four in their situations. It would not be appropriate for Nancy the Nurse to call several allies into a patient's room. Instead, she uses the second version of the Level Four script.

NANCY THE NURSE

PESKY PATIENT (ring, ring): "Hey, Nancy, come in here, I want a glass of juice. . . . My IV is running backward. . . . I need help reaching the phone."

NANCY: "I can't believe you, Mr. X, you have just done the impossible. I made a bet with my supervisor that you wouldn't do this to me anymore. She said, 'It'll take an act of God to keep his finger off that buzzer.' I said you wouldn't, and she said you would. Excuse me, I have to go tell her that she won the bet." Then Nancy gets out fast before there is any verbal reaction from the patient. Of course, it doesn't take a genius to figure out that this might not be appropriate for Nancy to use. It serves as an example, though, of the flexibility of using the script.

CARLOS THE CUSTOMER SERVICE REPRESENTATIVE

CUSTOMER (rave, rant, rant, rave and. . . .): "This blender is a piece of *& %$%&. I'll have you know I'm no sucker, you'll pay for this. . . ."

CARLOS: "Hey, Larry [plainclothes security guard], come over here. . . . Would you please repeat to Larry, here, exactly what you just said to me?"

This does draw attention to the manipulator, doesn't it?

Or take a look at another example of a different type. Consider an overworked government agency, for example. Because they find it difficult to keep up an accelerated pace, the employees may be as uptight as the customers that Carlos sees. In the following true incident, one author blew it royally. To quote:

Years ago, I walked into a government agency office to pick up a form that I needed. I had some doubts about whether they had this particular form on hand. My five-year-old and seven-year-old were in tow. When I came into the waiting room, there were at least sixty people sitting there holding numbers in their hands. My number turned out to be eighty-seven. It did not look like I was going to get out of there in this lifetime. I walked over to the window and asked if they did, in fact, have this particular form that I needed, before I waited all afternoon. I was assured that yes, they had that form. Go wait my turn. I spent the next two hours peeling my children off the laps of other people, off the walls, off the counter.

My number finally came up. I went to the window and asked for the form. I was told that the office did not have it. I would have to write away for it. "But, but," I said, "you assured me that you did. I wouldn't have waited here for two hours." The woman yelled, "Number eighty-eight." No apology. No excuse. I said, "But can't you get the form for me?" She responded, "Number eighty-eight, number eighty-eight." "Let me speak to the supervisor," I said through clenched teeth. "*I am the supervisor!*" she retorted. "Number eighty-eight."

Angry, feeling like a fool, and having wasted two stress-filled hours, I blew it: I screamed bloody murder. Sixty people including my children jumped two feet off their chairs.

While such a use of Level Four does focus a great deal of attention on the manipulator, we do not recommend this as a solution.

SEXY SHEILA

MALE CO-WORKER (RANDY) (in front of several employees): "Hey, Sam, I won the lotto! I get to spend the afternoon making it with Sheila in the boardroom."

SHEILA (chuckling to herself): "Oh, I can't wait to tell

her. I've gotta call her now!'' (She grabs a nearby phone and dials the weather number.) ''Hey, Sally, he did it again, you were right. I lost my bet, lunch is on me, yeah. . . . Yeah. . . . He sure did. . . . Yep. . . . Friday sounds great. . . . Gotta run, I'm late for a meeting.'' And Sheila disappears immediately afterward. [She has every right to disappear and go to her boss and report sexual harassment—and her boss then becomes the mediator.]

Can you imagine Sheila doing this? Do you have anywhere in your environment that Level Four could be successfully used?

CATHERINE AND HER COUSIN

ARCHIE: ''Those sons of————in Congress better not raise my taxes. Stupid idiots. Handing out money for welfare and unwed mothers. Bleeding hearts all of them. Pollution control, military expenditures. Just a bunch of hypocrites.''

CATHERINE: ''Pardon me, Archie, I've got to go use the phone. Cindy sure will be validated. . . . I mean, we had a bet—lunch at her favorite restaurant. I swore that you had changed; she said you hadn't. . . . Wonder where she'll want to go to lunch. . . .''

Catherine quickly exits to the next room, dials the weather number, and proceeds to talk to Cindy in a loud enough voice to be overheard: ''Yep, Archie did it again, just like you predicted. . . . Yep . . . yep. . . . I sure called this one wrong. . . . Anyway, where do you want to go to lunch? . . . Sounds great. . . . Friday at one. See you then. . . . Bye.''

Catherine then returns by way of the kitchen to pour some iced tea for Archie and herself. When she does reenter the room where Archie is, she immediately changes the topic to something that Archie will take off with and run, which could be almost anything.

However, if Archie should challenge her regarding her phone call: "What was that all about, that call to Cindy. What do ya mean you had a bet?"

Catherine then comes back with the *manipulator's* classic line, when cornered, "What do you mean, Archie? Doing what?"

Level Four lets the manipulator know that you know what is happening. Even though the manipulation may be largely subconscious, the revelation tends to raise the manipulator's awareness level in a hurry. The mere threat of a witness to this unacceptable verbal communication gives it the power to neutralize this encounter, as well as future manipulative attempts.

To extend our martial arts example, let's say your (physical) attacker comes up behind you and grabs your shoulders. You do not panic. You relax, but stay alert. As you are forgiving your assailant, you sink down, pulling your attacker with you. You grab the attacker's elbow and pull him or her off balance. The assailant is brought to the floor and you use various arm holds and locks to keep him or her there. The attacker is immobilized, and any attempt by the attacker to break the locks will result in a broken elbow.

The martial arts are exceedingly powerful. However, much of their success rests on the artist's ability to view an encounter with detachment and forgiveness. Successful use of the techniques for neutralizing manipulation requires an attitude change. Any jerk can get into a fistfight, and that usually is a waste of energy. A fight avoided is a fight won. Strength and might, alone, do not a winner make. And David slew Goliath.

Finally, to summarize Level Four:

1. You forgive.
2. You assess whether or not the manipulative attempt warrants calling attention to it by bringing in outside witness(es), real or fictitious.
3. You use your script so that the manipulator knows now that you know what is being attempted. And you draw attention to him or her in a big way.

We now move along to our last level, Level Five. Because Level Five is a more potent way of neutralizing manipulative attempts, and because it is somewhat more complex than the lower levels, it will be dealt with in two chapters, instead of only one.

CHAPTER 8

Reversal:
Level Five

A bit more study and analysis is required to use the reversal technique of Level Five. In our experience, manipulation succeeds primarily by using emotions (guilt and fear) as weapons. Therefore, in Level Five, it is important to ask yourself, "Exactly what emotion, or emotions, am I feeling with this attempted manipulation?" You feel slimed, but what is the gut reaction that you are experiencing? Guilt? Fear? Anger, as a result of guilt or fear? Embarrassment, as a result of guilt or fear? In order to stay relaxed, but alert, and to avoid getting emotional during an encounter, it helps to identify your reaction. If you do this often enough, it serves as a vaccine, or inoculation, that helps prevent you from automatically counterattacking.

Next you need to ask yourself, "Why is the manipulator trying to manipulate me?" Obviously, he or she wants some of your power. The more specific you can be, the greater will be your understanding of the unpleasant event, and hence, your ability to neutralize this encounter and future manipulative attempts. Knowing *why* someone is trying to do this to you lets you be more forgiving, more gracious, and less controlled by *other* people's inferiority complexes.

Nancy the Nurse's former patient is in a strange environment. He feels scared and helpless and powerless.

A child from a broken home envies Tess with her friends and confidence.

Annie the Airhead is a free spirit, confident, and enjoying life. This can be a bummer, for example, to someone going through a midlife crisis.

The hotel guest feels that he has to humiliate Fred the Front Desk Manager because, chances are, he really envies him and his perceived power. There, in a luxury hotel, the hotel guest can be a big shot.

Marcy's mom is terrified of not being needed anymore by her daughter. She makes a big deal out of how busy she is and how much she sacrifices for Marcy.

Attila the Hun reached his level of incompetence long ago and is afraid now that one of his employees may take his job. He feels threatened.

Clara the Closet Apologizer, probably has no place in her life where she has any semblance of power. The only way that she can feel important is by trying to make a fool out of Martin or someone else.

The men who try to manipulate Sexy Sheila with stupid or suggestive comments are probably having a rough time dealing with a businesswoman in the first place, let alone a very pretty one. Their masculinity, their sense of power, and their sexuality get all mixed up.

Archie, Catherine's cousin, is coming from a point of such fear and insecurity that he resembles the neighborhood bully.

Carlos takes a daily dose of verbal abuse from fearful customers. They fear that they are real schmucks for buying something that quickly fell apart. They fear that they may have lost their money. They fear what their spouses will say if they don't get the problem resolved. Fear then taps into their whole closet of anxieties and they flip over to anger. Then every single time in their lives that they were ripped off, cheated, or made to look like a fool comes to vivid life. They show up at Carlos's desk ready to punch his face in. He represents their whole life story of ain't-life-unfair.

("Hey, Mabel, remember that time you sent away for the plastic broccoli centerpiece, and they never sent it to you? And they went out of business before we got our money back?" "Sure do, Roger," Mabel replies. "Remember the time I bought that carton of eggs, and when I got it home from the store, one was broken? Remember what I did? I got in the car and I drove the twenty-five miles back to Herkimer's General Store, I did. . . .")

Manipulation includes an element of fantasy. Because its success relies on ephemeral concepts (like the ghosts of guilt and fear from our past or in our anxiety closet), it is a bit like a dream. And like a dream, it is part fantasy.

The sand castle that you built yesterday at the ocean's edge (complete with moat) was very real and would last forever. Today it exists only in your memory. Likewise, manipulation has elements of both reality and fantasy.

Therefore, with Level Five you are going to take the fantasy of the manipulation and make it real. You actually must take the manipulation and run with it. You focus a lot of attention on it. You make it *all* real. You magnify it. You play with it.

Level Five can be most interesting.

By neutralizing instead of counterattacking, you are giving the manipulators the opportunity to correct themselves, to stop the manipulative behavior, and to get off your back.

Now you must make the fantasy real. You will learn to take the negative energy of the manipulation itself and send the same negative energy back to the manipulator. If you do this successfully, the manipulator will feel exactly as he or she tried (but did not succeed) to make you feel. With neutralization, the negative force of the assailant is used against the assailant. You do not generate any of your own negative energy. Neutralization is not counterattack. We will show you the difference shortly.

In Level One, you deaf both the manipulator and the manipulation. In Level Two, you ignore the manipulation but pay friendly attention to the manipulator. In Level Three, you confront the manipulator regarding the manipulation by vulnerably telling him or her how you feel. You either dispel the manipulation or give your permission to the manipulator to continue manipulating, but alone, without you. And remember: *Strength through vulnerability is fortified by forgiveness.* In Level Four, you and your real or fictitious cohorts focused attention on the manipulator. Now, in Level Five, you focus full blast on *both* the manipulation *and* the manipulator.

REMEMBER THAT MANY MANIPULATIONS AND MANIPULATIVE ATTEMPTS ARE BEING EXECUTED ON A SUBCONSCIOUS LEVEL BY THE MANIPULATOR.

Shortly, we will look at Level Five using the same characters as before. Please keep in mind that the manipulator in each example is really paying our character a compliment. The manipulator perceives our character as having more power than he or she does.

As you read each example, remember to try Levels One through Four (where appropriate), and see if those levels do the trick. Please realize that going around Level-Fiving people when it is not called for will make you a lonely person. It is powerful. It can be destructive if not used carefully. Remember earlier when we mentioned that you don't want to slam someone down on the mat when he or she only tapped you on the shoulder to ask directions?

We will now do the first pass through Level Five with each of our characters. Then, in Chapter 9, we will make another pass using our characters with Level Five techniques again, to show you a somewhat different response (more or less exaggerated). The double pass is intended to leave you with a greater understanding of how the fantasy elements are identified and magnified, and how the reversal occurs.

ANNIE THE AIRHEAD

Fantasy: Annie is incompetent, childish, an airhead, a ditz.
Reality: Annie is a competent employee enjoying life. She would enjoy it even more without the verbal abuse.

CO-WORKER: "Hey, Annie, how many Annies does it take to change a light bulb?"

ANNIE (in a weepy tone): "I didn't know it still showed like this. . . . Two years of psychotherapy down the drain. . . . All that time and money to make me appear normal . . . so people wouldn't make fun of me (wail). . . . I'm a loser, I'm an airhead."

Well, the manipulator did not expect that response. This was the level that Annie actually used in real life. And it neutralized the manipulators once and for all. By the time Annie completed her spiel (complete with crocodile tears), the manipulators in the office were falling all over themselves to apologize to Annie. They felt guilty and just plain awful. Did Annie send the energy of the manipulation back onto the manipulator? You bet. Now the manipulators feel slimed. See how it works? Interesting, huh? Did Annie actually have two years of psychotherapy for being an airhead? No. She was simply acting out the manipulator's fantasy.

Annie had to examine what the manipulator wanted. This was easy to do since the manipulations were a continuing phenomenon. Her power, her free spirit, her confidence in herself were obvious. They wanted to put her down. Annie decided that both guilt (How can anyone have enough fun with life to waltz through it, and do it with pink bows in her hair?) and fear (of ridicule) were being used as weapons.

While Annie did not diagram every insult, she quickly recognized *the intent* of the insults: She was abnormal, an airhead, floating through life. Because she was not paying her dues, that is, feeling guilty and burdened with inferiority, she was to be made fun of, punished, and insulted.

So Annie took this absurd fantasy and made it real. In a scene straight from Broadway, she became a card-carrying airhead, seeking help for this rare condition. Can the manipulators ever be sure that Annie was not pulling their legs? Maybe. Maybe not. It worked, though, and Annie's life in the office improved one hundred percent.

MARCY AND HER MOM

Fantasy: Marcy is inconsiderate to impose on her mother in this way. Marcy is selfish. Mom is worthless now to Marcy, and no longer needed, since Marcy has her own family to nurture.

Reality: Mom is bored silly and lives to see her grandchildren. She'd give anything to play an even bigger part in Marcy's life. Marcy still needs her Mom's support and loves her. Marcy is actively trying to insure that her parents have quality time with their grandchildren.

MOM: "Marcy, you know I'd love to watch the kids for you next Saturday, but that was the only evening that your father and I had planned to stay home and be together . . . but never mind, that's okay, we'll be happy to cancel our plans and do it." (That same dialogue has happened every time Marcy has called—Mom is bored silly. Don't start feeling sorry for Mom.)

MARCY: "Oh, Mom, I do use you and Dad so. . . . I'm such a selfish daughter, taking time away from your busy schedule, to see your grandkids. Tell you what, I'll get Tess down the street to baby-sit. That way you'll have the evening for yourselves. . . . No, Mom, I insist. Tess will do just great. . . . Maybe next time you'll be freer."

Mom sure did not expect that, especially since she lives to see the kids.

Marcy just didn't want the guilt trips any longer. She asked herself, "What is Mom saying? What is Mom's fantasy?" Mom is trying to convince her that Mom is important and busy, since she is terrified that Marcy doesn't need her anymore. (Marcy still does.) And she is trying to make Marcy feel guilty because she has a family of her own now, inconsiderate daughter that she's become!

So Marcy, in Level Five, makes this fantasy come true. Mom is too busy to watch the kids. Marcy is an inconsiderate daughter. Marcy will hire a sitter.

Marcy did not take on the manipulative energy. Mom got it right back, and it feels terrible. However, Marcy did not have to use Level Five on her Mom, since Level Two worked nicely. This example is included only as an illustration.

TESS THE PRETEEN

Fantasy: Tess is a wimp. She deserves to be put down, humiliated. She is not as strong as the bullies who taunt her.

Reality: Tess is pretty, Tess is smart, and Tess has friends. Tess is reading a book on how to stop manipulation!

FELLOW STUDENT: "Hey, Tess, who buys your clothes . . . the school principal?"

TESS: "Well, yes, in fact, Mr. Jones and I went shopping yesterday afternoon. He helped me enormously. Were you wondering if he'd take you? I bet he would if you asked him nicely."

With Tess, the manipulator is trying to reduce her status and make her look like a nerd, dweeb, or geek. He or she is threatened by Tess's confidence, friends, and enjoyment of life. The fellow student wants some of Tess's power. Usually, a manipulator in this circumstance will use fear—fear of humiliation, fear of standing out in a crowd, peer pressure.

PEER PRESSURE IS RAW MANIPULATION.

The manipulator is saying to Tess, "I'm calling you a nerd/dweeb/geek. What are you going to do about it?" He is expecting Tess to say, "I'm *not* a nerd/dweeb/geek" and get into an argument. The manipulator hopes to reduce Tess to tears.

Tess simply says, "Gee, I guess I *am* a nerd/dweeb/geek. I asked my principal's advice with clothes shopping." This is not what the manipulator expected to hear. Do you believe that Tess really went clothes shopping with Mr. Jones?

"You want to paint me as a nerd/dweeb/geek. All right, I'll be a nerd/dweeb/geek for you." And the manipulator knows the rules have been changed. The manipulator can come back and say, "Hey, Tess admits she's a nerd/dweeb/geek." But since nerds/dweebs/geeks don't admit to it, that in itself is a contradiction, isn't it?

So at the least, the manipulator feels uncomfortable, Tess leaves feeling fine, and everyone else is slightly confused. But next time the manipulator will search out someone else to manipulate and leave Tess alone. She is too unpredictable. And the manipulator may even approach her in a more kindly way in the future.

Please keep in mind that there is seldom only one correct reply for any given negative verbal experience. If there were a different reply for each possible kind of manipulation, you'd die of old age trying to memorize all of the correct answers. Tess and all of the other characters here could use Level Five techniques in different ways. The bottom line is the same, however. The fantasy is made real. The manipulation is neutralized.

FRED THE FRONT DESK MANAGER

Fantasy: Fred is a jerk. He can be grabbed by the——on a subject he'll never discuss—his own mortality.

Reality: Fred is not a jerk. He holds a responsible position and does a great job. He can discuss anything in public, even his own mortality.

HOTEL GUEST: "Hey, Fred, how old are you?"

FRED: "Forty-seven."

HOTEL GUEST: "I never knew a guy named Fred to live past the age of fifty."

FRED: "What's your name?"

HOTEL GUEST: "Clyde."

FRED: "Clyde, you've got me worried now. When I get off work, I'll call my doctor first thing to make an appointment. Then I'll call my priest. Thanks for sharing that with me."

Fred says this as if he genuinely means it. He says this in the same tone he would use if he had just found out that the dog that bit him had rabies.

This manipulator is a real wise guy who gets his jollies by shooting down people in public whom he inwardly envies or admires. He perceives that Fred has a lot of power, while he, the manipulator, does not. Fred's prematurely white hair is a sensitive spot with Fred. Fred's hands are tied (he can't go over and choke the guy, as much as he'd like to). Everyone is listening at this point. And, like many of us, Fred does not enjoy being publicly embarrassed.

The manipulator, who is trying to set the rules, is counting on Fred's fear of arguing about his mortality in front of a group of people. The manipulator hopes that Fred will be speechless. If Fred isn't speechless, the manipulator is at least counting on Fred coming back with the standard retort of "Oh, yeah? I'll outlive you, buddy."

The manipulator is not prepared for Fred to take the fantasy elements of the attempted manipulation and turn them into reality. As if diagraming a sentence, Fred instantly (just as you are learning to do) says to himself, "This man is trying to make me afraid that I will die soon."

Fred recognized the weapon (fear). He identified the fantasy in the manipulation. He made it real. He told the guest he would see his doctor, call his priest, and thanked him very much for the information. Now, of course, we all know that Fred is not going to call his doctor, or his priest. Can the manipulator be sure? Could the energy of the manipulation be coming back to haunt him? Could other people be snickering? Has the manipulator lost control of his own game? Yes. The rules changed somewhere along the way, didn't they? This was not what the manipulator expected. The fantasy was made real. The manipulation was neutralized.

DAVE WHO WORKS FOR ATTILA THE HUN

Fantasy: Dave is incompetent.
Reality: Dave is so competent that Attila is threatened by him.

ATTILA/BOSS (handing Dave a whole week's worth of work): "I want this done by noon."
DAVE (enthusiastically): "Okeydokey . . . no sweat, I'll have it done by noon."
(Noon comes . . . da da Da DA!)
ATTILA/BOSS: "I thought you said you were to get this done by noon. You're not finished. . . ."
DAVE: "Gosh, Boss, I thought I could get it done. I'm so disappointed in myself. I must be slipping. I mean, I really thought I could get it done by now."
Since Dave has been manipulated successfully in the past, Attila does not expect this reversal. The rules are changed to Dave's advantage. Evidence is strong that the boss does not want to fire Dave. He's probably not that stupid. The high-quality work coming out of his office (that is, Dave's work) has raised his status within the company. He doesn't want to kill Dave, he wants to keep him alive

and well so he can manipulate him further. Disclaimer: If Attila, in fact, is so stupid that he considers firing him, then Dave might want to consider the alternative response given in the next chapter.

MARTIN THE CLUB MEMBER

Fantasy: Martin is a dimwit.
Reality: Martin saw Clara. Martin is right.

CLARA: "That wasn't me you saw downtown, Martin."
MARTIN: "Ooops, me and my big mouth. Sorry, Clara."
CLARA: "But it *wasn't me.*"
MARTIN: "You're right, it wasn't Clara, everybody, it wasn't Clara." (Wink, wink.)

Here you are complying with this absurd fantasy. Clara is trying to embarrass Martin publicly. Could Clara now be the one feeling embarrassed? Everyone is staring at her and snickering. Just what was Clara really doing downtown this morning? What is she trying to hide? Could the Closet Apologizer herself now be experiencing some of the energy of the put-down? Most likely.

In the remaining examples, we will further explore the process of how reversal works. You, as readers, will learn to recognize the fantasy quickly and follow several basic rules that are simple and easy to remember. As you practice them, they will become automatic.

HERE ARE THE GUIDELINES

The manipulation attempt comes zinging your way. You start to feel that ol' slimy feeling and say to yourself: "This person is trying to manipulate me . . . trying to control how I think, feel, or behave.''

1. Forgive. This is the golden rule for handling manipulators. It is the golden rule for all five levels. You are the one with the greater power. It is a compliment that the manipulator has chosen *you*. You are the one now playing this game, using your rules. You have the strength to choose compassion over counterattack. Remember, only a coward never forgives.
2. Ask yourself what weapon is being used against you. This helps you identify the fantasy. What is your opponent trying to make you feel?
3. If it is guilt, immediately turn off the self-imposed guilt button. Tell yourself not to take on this responsibility.
4. If you feel fear/anger rising, tell yourself that this is not the time or the place to afford yourself the luxury of becoming emotional. It is important to keep your emotions neutral in order to counter this manipulation successfully.
5. What is the fantasy, what is the dare? Be specific. For example, the fantasy might be identified as being that Fred the Front Desk Manager won't discuss his mortality in front of the guests and employees in the hotel lobby; or that Dave won't discuss his productivity. You know that the manipulators are daring you to call them on their outrageous behavior—but in what *specific* area? What subject matter?
6. Don't feel guilty and kick yourself if you used Level One, Two, Three, or Four to counter a manipulation successfully and then, three hours later, twigged on the perfect Level Five that you might have used.

To summarize, think of Level Five as *The Four F's:* FORGIVE; ask yourself, What do I FEEL (guilt or fear/ anger)? What is the FANTASY? Make that fantasy FAN-TASTIC. Forgive, feel, fantasy, *fantastic* fantasy.

The Four F's:

1. FORGIVE!
2. FEELING what? Guilt or fear/anger? (Helps you locate the fantasy.)
3. What is the FANTASY?
4. Make the fantasy really FANTASTIC!

With reversal, you make the fantasy real. If you execute it properly, the manipulator receives back the exact same amount of negative energy as he or she tried to give you. None of it remains on you. Let's illustrate the Four F's with our characters.

NANCY THE NURSE

Fantasy: This patient can complain to Nancy's supervisor and get her into trouble (fear). Nancy is rotten, not helping this patient (guilt).

Reality: Nancy is a fine nurse, but she is not assigned to this room.

PATIENT (ring, ring): "Hey, Nancy, come in here, I want a glass of juice. . . . My IV is running backward. . . . My bedpan is overflowing. . . . I can't reach the phone." (The family is sitting around.)

Nancy does the Four F's:

1. FORGIVE him, he is a sick man.
2. What do I FEEL? Fear. He could complain to my supervisor.
3. What is one of the FANTASIES here? That he'll get me in trouble.
4. I will make that fantasy real in a FANTASTIC way.

NANCY: "Have any of you mentioned I've been in here, taking care of you? I got a call from my supervisor ...no explanation.... I'm to report to her right after work."

PATIENT: "Well, I don't think I've said anything, why?"

NANCY: "Well, I'm in deep trouble now. I've been written up three times so far for taking care of other nurse's patients, and they told me I'd be fired if I got written up again. Oh, Lord, how am I going to pay the rent? Does your company need an experienced R.N.?"

Nancy knows she is being manipulated. Nancy knows the patient is using fear: Nancy can't be rude to him or he'll tattle on her and she'll get in trouble. The patient is also using guilt—she's a rotten nurse not to help a sick person. Both dares ... both fantasies.

So Nancy makes the fantasy real. Except, instead of Nancy feeling fearful, now the patient feels fearful and maybe a little guilty. Except, instead of Nancy worrying about getting into trouble, he's worried she is going to lose her job—and it is all his fault. The chances are high that he will not expect her to cater to his every whim in the future.

CARLOS THE CUSTOMER SERVICE
REPRESENTATIVE

Fantasy: Carlos is personally responsible for the broken blender. Carlos will get into a lot of trouble over this one, you'd better believe it.

Reality: Carlos is doing his best. He is not responsible for the blender. Carlos isn't any the happier because the man feels hassled about the blender.

CUSTOMER: "This blender is a piece of *& %$#. I'll have you know I'm no sucker, you'll pay for this. . . ."

Carlos does the Four F's:

1. FORGIVE.
2. The FEELING is fear.
3. The FANTASY—is I'm fearful he'll get me in trouble.
4. FANTASTIC FANTASY—he can't get me in trouble, I'm already fired!

CARLOS: "Oh, I can't believe this. . . . I'm gonna lose my job. I'll get you a new Sunbeam; it'll work. It doesn't matter now. I'm out of here. I'm responsible for ordering your brand in the first place. My boss told me, 'You screw up one more time, Carlos, and you're history.' And the wife, she's expecting a baby . . . and the rent's overdue. Where do you work?"

CUSTOMER: "Acme Corporation. Why?"

CARLOS: "Maybe you could help me get a job there?"

Let's be frank. Level Five is seldom appropriate in customer service situations. However, in order to observe Level Five in action, let's continue: Carlos is not paid enough to take this type of verbal abuse. People who come into the store and are ready to punch his face in need to understand that their behavior is not cool. It is hoped that, because Carlos counters this manipulation, the customer will think twice about doing the same thing another time.

Carlos realizes the fantasy: The customer is acting as if I, Carlos, am personally responsible for his busted blender. His dare is that if I don't cower, he'll have my job. So Carlos makes this fantasy come true. Carlos is responsible for the busted blender. He ordered them. He doesn't have to worry about losing his job; he's already lost it. Now the customer can feel the guilt and fear. Are you beginning to understand how the energy is transferred back onto the manipulator? Let's apply it step by step with Sexy Sheila.

SEXY SHEILA

Fantasy: Sheila is a dumb broad, who is public property because she is so sexy. No one has the right to look like that and try to be in management, in a man's world.

Reality: Sheila is trained in business management. She is not public property. She is a sensitive human being and a good manager.

MALE CO-WORKER (RANDY) (in front of several employees): "Hey, Sam, I won the lotto. I get to spend the afternoon making it with Sheila in the boardroom."

Sheila does the Four F's:

1. FORGIVE.
2. The FEELING is fear and guilt.
3. The FANTASY is that I'm available to any creep that wants to put his hands on me.
4. FANTASTIC FANTASY—I'll let him know that I'm just dying for his love.

SHEILA (in a serious tone): "Randy, you really know how to hurt a gal. I had oysters Rockefeller for lunch and I am horny. I'd love to spend the afternoon in the boardroom with you. Arnold Schwarzenegger is nothing compared with you, Randy. However, I have to run the income statement for Acme. What a bummer!"

Does Randy now look cool in front of the other men and women in the office? Does Randy have oysters Rockefeller on his face? Do you believe that Sheila is upset because she can't spend the afternoon in the boardroom with Randy?

What is the fantasy? What is the dare? As mentioned before, the men are daring Sheila to discuss her sexuality and her vulnerability. They probably feel she is afraid of public humiliation. So what does Sheila do? She confronts her sexuality and makes it real, publicly. She is horny. She ate oysters—that proves it. She'd give up Arnold Schwarzenneger any day to have Randy. Now if Randy and the others truly believe this, then she should look for another job. This corporation will not go far.

CATHERINE AND HER COUSIN

First, a little background. Archie, you know, is obnoxious as he can be. He resembles the neighborhood bully. He is coming from a point of fear (out of control) since he has had numerous five- to six-digit medical bills. He is retired and is literally being kept alive by modern medical technology for his various serious ailments. He is on Medicare. He is in and out of the hospital more times than the chief of staff.

He rages on during every visit to Catherine's house. He is insulting and abusive. By implication, he dares Catherine to throw him out the door. He dares her to confront his tirades against anything that most people consider decent.

So what is the fantasy? The fantasy is that he is powerful, he is threatening, and he has complete control. But what specific fantasy does he convey regarding his own circumstance? That he can look death straight in the face forever. Move over, Agent 007/Indiana Jones. The reality is that he is scared, weak, and out of control. And he acts mean.

Catherine needs to make the fantasy real. Let's make it real. Archie will have all the control and power that he wants in order to handle something that terrifies him. . . . Which is? His own helplessness. Because he is dependent on the very institutional and social structures that he condemns.

Fantasy: Archie will live forever. Archie can control everything and everyone. And Archie's behavior and outbursts will be tolerated because *He Is Family.*

Reality: Archie is a mess. He is terrified of death. He is totally dependent on others. He is acting like a bully. He belongs in counseling.

ARCHIE: ''Those sons of————in Congress won't raise my taxes! I'll sue 'em! Stupid idiots! Handing out money for welfare and unwed mothers! Bleeding hearts all of them! Pollution control, military expenditures. Just a bunch of hypocrites!''

Catherine does the Four F's:

1. FORGIVE.
2. I FEEL fear.
3. The FANTASY is that he can control anyone and anything.
4. FANTASTIC FANTASY: Fine, let Archie run Congress.

CATHERINE: "You know, Archie, you might want to contact your representative. I understand Congress is trying to control rising medical costs—by withholding or greatly reducing the money spent on catastrophic illness for the elderly. There is a proposal in Congress now. I'd write my congressman and senator to check on it if I were you."

Suddenly Archie has problems. It is not just rhetorical. Archie may have to cough up $75,000 for his next operation, money he does not have. He'll contact his congressman and his senators, you can rest assured. He'll be too busy writing letters to harass Catherine. And he is terrified.

Can you see how Catherine refused the energy and gave it back to Archie to worry about?

As mentioned before, there is never just one answer that fits the circumstance. Using these techniques is more an attitude change than a matter of memorizing pat responses. You can play with the manipulation; you can play with the manipulator. But using your own set of rules instead of the manipulator's set. You are the one in control, because the manipulator wants some of your power.

In the next chapter, we will see our characters again using Level Five, with different responses.

CHAPTER 9

Reversal Revisited: More Level Five

Soon we will illustrate Level Five again using the same characters, but with different responses. Before we do, let's take a look at the concepts of brutal honesty, counterattack (a no-no), and the use of the word "should" (the "S" word—a guaranteed guilt producer).

"HONESTLIES"

"Honestlies" is pronounced like the word honestly in the plural, or it may be broken down into the two words, "Honest Lies." It is a noun, and it is used to describe brutal honesty. Since Level Five is the most severe of the five levels, you may be forced to use it when dealing with one of the most unpleasant manipulations that you can encounter—that is, brutal honesty. Since honestlies are such vicious manipulations, they often warrant a high level to neutralize them.

Has this ever happened to you? Someone says something that truly hurts, and then says, "I just wanted to be honest with you." This person is a manipulator. This is a circumstance where some distorted version of the truth is used as a weapon. How do you feel when someone uses honestlies on you? You feel guilty and/or fearful, don't you?

"Why, they were just being honest with me. I can't stop them from being honest. I must be some kind of awful person if I don't let them be honest with me."

Now you feel guilt and/or fear because of what the truth may be (however perverted the manipulator's statement actually is). We feel that that is a wicked thing to do to someone.

A married acquaintance of ours, a counselor, simply decided one day that she wanted to play the field, have many boyfriends, and travel, but not get a divorce. She explained to her husband that she "just needed to do this to actualize herself." Her husband was stunned to say the least.

Eventually she came back to her husband and told him how much better she felt, how much better her communications with her clients were now, and how self-actualized she had become. When asked how her husband was taking all this, she said, "Boy, is he bummed out. He just can't communicate with me anymore. Did I do something wrong?" Absolutely nothing, right? She was *only* doing *brutal honesty*. Implicitly she had gone to her husband and said, "Hey, look, this is how I feel, you wouldn't want me to lie to you, would you?" It is too bad that he couldn't have gotten a restraining order against her at that point.

If someone hurts you by using honestlies, you can generally disbelieve whatever they tell you, because they are using it to hurt you.

The authors are not recommending *dis*honesty, nor are we suggesting shutting off open and truthful communications. The two interactions that follow show the difference between open communication and honestlies. We suspect that you will understand the difference and appreciate what we are trying to communicate.

Open Communication

John: "Bite my head off, why don't you, Mary!"

Mary: "I'm sorry I snapped at you, John. I'm feeling pretty scared right now about the surgery tomorrow. Please forgive me." (Mary is being truthful, apologetic, and vulnerable.)

John: "That's okay, Mary, I know you're worried. I'll try to keep as much of the stress off of you as I can. Hey, you'll do just fine tomorrow."

Versus Honestlies

Sue: "You really should drop twenty pounds, Harold, you'd feel so much better, and look terrific. Hey, I'm just being honest. I worry about you, I honestly do." (Notice the "S" word at the beginning—"should." It usually guarantees that an *un*healthy dose of guilt will follow.)

Another honestlie:

Sue: "You shouldn't eat those eggs, Harold; they are bad for your cholesterol level. Honestly, you'd think you didn't care whether you checked out on me, or what! I really love you Harold. I'm just telling you this honestly for your own good."

Level Five is not counterattack.

Here, at Level Five, it becomes easier and easier to analyze the fantasy, figure out where the opponent is coming from, and sidestep the main goal of manipulation. When it becomes easy, you, the reader, may be tempted to take this information and counterattack instead of attempting to neutralize. While counterattacking during a high-level manipulation can be heady, it defeats its own purpose because *you* end up looking like the *bad guy*. This can lead to your feeling guilty, and your having to apologize, and on and on ad nauseam.

In the following example, try to identify which responses are counterattack, and which are neutralizing or countering manipulation. The feeling that you get in the pit of your stomach is your validation of which ones are which.

You go to a family reunion and everyone is there. You are sensitive about growing old (just like Fred). Your very overweight cousin asks you, "Did you just get another face lift?" Everyone is staring at you. Choose your reply:

A: "Did *you* just gain twenty-five more pounds?"

B: "Yep, the twentieth one was free."

C: "It beats liposuction."

D: "Yep, the surgeon is the most eligible guy in town. By the fortieth face-lift, he'll be *all mine.*"

Which responses truly disarm the manipulator? And leave you looking good? Which responses are effective for neutralization and why? Why are they effective? Can you see where answers B and D identify the dare and magnify it for a mini Level Five type response? Anyway, that was a crummy thing the cousin said.

THE "S" WORD (SHOULD) OR HOW TO DEAL WITH "SHOULDLIES"

There is no need for a long discourse here. "Should" is a bad word. It's very existence is an anathema (a thing to be damned). Webster's Dictionary: "Should: obligation, duty, propriety, necessity. . . . (Children should be loved)." How much more guilt can you get than that? Even the dictionary makes you feel guilty. Of course, you *should* love them. Anyone but a creep should love his or her children. Do you love your children *enough?* Do you really want to feel guilty? See what we mean? The word *should* implies guilt. It is the "S" word. Shouldlies are awful. We should be a better employee. We should be a better parent. We should love our family more. We should give more to charitable causes. We should pay more attention to our health. We should try to reduce our cholesterol. It goes on indefinitely. Just recognize that another version of the Brutal Honestlies is being played out when you encounter shouldlies.

In Level Five, the manipulative energy, following the principles of the soft (unarmed) martial arts, comes back on the manipulator, full circle, leaving the intended victim unharmed. If handled correctly, it lets the manipulator receive back the exact degree of negative energy that he or she tried to impose on the victim in the first place. The intended victim turns the energy around in such a way that the manipulators punch themselves out with their own fists—their own negative energy.

The motto for Level Five is as follows: If you think this fits me, let's see how it looks on you!

Let's discuss Level Five in terms of the martial arts.

Suppose you are walking down the street. Your assailant, a large man, rushes up to you and grabs your arm. You become alert but totally relaxed. You maintain eye contact. The normal reaction (before you changed the rules) would be for you to dig in your heels as the attacker attempts to pull you toward him.

Now, however, you do just the opposite. You pull your attacker *toward you* with your free hand, locking his elbow and immobilizing his other arm. As his forward momentum (now off balance) propels him toward you, you raise your knee, taking your foot off the ground. As he crashes down, his groin takes his full weight as it lands on your knee.

Here the attacker's energy has been turned against him to neutralize his aggressive behavior.

Let's use our characters again to illustrate Level Five, whether appropriate or not, so that you can see more of the reversal in action.

ANNIE THE AIRHEAD

CO-WORKER: "Hey, Annie, how many Annies does it take to change a light bulb?"

Annie does the Four F's:

1. FORGIVE.
2. FEELING fear and some guilt.
3. FANTASY—I'm an airhead.
4. FANTASTIC FANTASY—I'm a really *dumb* airhead.

ANNIE: "Oh, Alan, . . . er, is there a light bulb that needs to be changed?" [I'm so ditzy, I don't even understand the insult.]

MARCY AND HER MOM

MOM: "Marcy, you know I'd love to watch the kids for you next Saturday, but that was the one evening that your father and I had planned to stay home and be together . . . but never mind, that's okay, we'll be happy to cancel our plans and do it."

Marcy does the Four F's:

1. FORGIVE.
2. FEELING guilt.
3. FANTASY—Mom's too busy and I'm always imposing.

4. FANTASTIC FANTASY—She'll no longer have to worry about the kids, period.

MARCY: "Oh, Mom, you are so busy now and doing so many things—truly living life. You don't need the headache of baby-sitting the grandkids anymore. I've hired Tess down the street to baby-sit *every* weekend and *every* day after school to help me. Let us know when you and Dad finally get caught up. Maybe we can arrange a mutual time for you to see the kids."

This is *really* overkill. If Marcy said that to her mom, she'd probably faint.

TESS THE PRETEEN

FELLOW STUDENT: "Hey, Tess, that's the same shirt you wore yesterday. Hey, everybody, look at Tess."

Tess does the Four F's:

1. FORGIVE.
2. FEELING fear—being embarrassed in front of others.
3. FANTASY—I'm a pitiful, powerless, little person who can't wear a new T-shirt every day.
4. FANTASTIC FANTASY—I am powerless! Look at this situation—totally hopeless!

TESS: "Yeah, talk about the pits—my Mom's on strike and the washer's busted!"

Children's manipulations are hard to counter using Level Five. The social pecking order and the often vicious nature of the manipulations are intertwined. It is often difficult to pull a Level Five out of thin air, instantly, in response to a one-shot insult. One-shots are harder to neutralize than continuing manipulations in the home or in the office, because they are less predictable. Tess can probably accomplish more by using Levels One through Four, and by using humor wherever possible.

For instance, Tess was annoyed when the school bully kept looking over at her computer monitor and obviously plagiarizing her work. So she just started typing, "Hey, Johnny, I'll just copy this disk for you. It will be easier on your neck that way."

FRED THE FRONT DESK MANAGER

The following response, made in real life by Fred, accomplished its purpose. The hotel guest was so embarrassed that he looked as if he wanted to dig a hole and crawl in.

GUEST: "Hey, Fred, how old are you?"

FRED: "Forty-seven."

HOTEL GUEST: "I never knew a guy named Fred to live past the age of fifty."

Fred does the Four F's:

1. FORGIVE the jerk.
2. I am feeling FEAR of public embarrassment.
3. The FANTASY is that I won't discuss my mortality, something this personal, in front of an audience.
4. I'll make this FANTASTIC fantasy real. Yes, I'll discuss it, and boy, he won't like it!

FRED: "That's an awful thing to say to someone with a terminal disease."

Fred was not lying. He didn't say that *he* had a terminal disease. He made a flat statement. When he said it in that manner, however, no one doubted for one minute that he referred to himself. The energy was delivered back to the manipulator in the exact degree that it had been sent to Fred by the manipulator. Fred recognized that it was a manipulation. He recognized the weapon: fear. He recognized the fantasy: He is trying to make me afraid that I will die soon. Also, he is daring me to discuss this in front of a bunch of strangers and employees in the lobby. So I'll surprise him. *I will discuss my mortality in such a way that he'll end up wishing he had never brought it up in the first place.*

This is how Fred does the above comeback, fast: Slimy feeling. Fear. He is implying that I look so old I'm ready to die. I'll discuss that in front of everyone. I'll make the fantasy come true in an exaggerated fashion.

DAVE WHO WORKS FOR ATTILA THE HUN

ATTILA/BOSS (after giving Dave an impossible workload): "You aren't done. You said you'd get this finished by noon. Why aren't you done with it?"

Dave does the Four F'S:

1. FORGIVE.
2. FEELING fear.
3. FANTASY is that he'll fire me. For what? Low productivity—that's the *real* fantasy!
4. I'll make it a FANTASTIC FANTASY: I'll make his dreams come true! I'm a goldbricker, and I'm out of here thanks to personnel and their liberal transfer policy.

DAVE: "You must consider me a very nonproductive employee. I'll make an appointment with Personnel and see if they can transfer me to another department—one that, hopefully, can make use of my other talents."

Well, this is exactly what the boss does *not* want to hear. Why, Personnel will ask, does he want a transfer? Well, he'll explain, the boss gave him 300 pages of financial reports to analyze in three hours and he couldn't do it. He is nonproductive. He only did 287 pages.

Now who looks stupid? Dave? Hardly. Attila looks like the slave driver he is. Dave made the fantasy *fantastically* real. So real that he would go to Personnel about his incompetence.

MARTIN THE CLUB MEMBER

CLARA: "That wasn't me you saw downtown, Martin." Martin does the Four F'S:

1. FORGIVE.
2. FEELING what? Fear (embarrassment).
3. FANTASY—She's making me look like a fool.
4. FANTASTIC FANTASY—I'll be a total fool. I'll let her whole undercover operation out in the open.

MARTIN (very seriously): "I'm sorry, Clara, I'm so very sorry. You have a right to your privacy. I never should have told your husband I saw you."

NANCY THE NURSE

PESKY PATIENT (ring, ring): "Hey, Nancy, come in here. I want a glass of juice. . . . My IV is running backwards. . . . My bedpan is overflowing. . . . I need help reaching the phone."

Nancy does the Four F'S:

1. FORGIVE.
2. FEELING guilty. Why? What's the fantasy?
3. FANTASY is that I'm a bad nurse not to care for him.
4. FANTASTIC FANTASY: I'm a really *bad* nurse.

NANCY: ''Mr. X, did I tell you about the time that I got thrown out of nursing school? I mean it took me seven years and four schools till I got my degree. (This is said while she drops the bedpan ''accidentally'' on the floor.) Ooops. That ol' Nancy, always in the Ooops Box. Anyway, as I was saying, my parents were so proud of me. . . . (Backs up and tips over the IV stand.) Oh my, clumsy Nancy. . . . Hope the supervisor doesn't come by. She's still mad about my giving that guy the wrong meds last night. . . . You know all the excitement it caused. . . . CPR. . . . Where was I?''

This dialogue could go on indefinitely. You get the picture, though. Now the patient can worry or be afraid of what she could do to him while trying to help speed along his recovery.

CARLOS THE CUSTOMER SERVICE REPRESENTATIVE

CUSTOMER: ''This blender is a piece of *& %$ &. I'll have you know I'm no sucker, you'll pay for this. . . .''
Carlos does the Four F'S:

1. FORGIVE.
2. FEELING guilt. Why? What's the fantasy?
3. FANTASY—I, personally, am responsible for his blender breaking. It's all my fault.
4. FANTASTIC FANTASY—I designed this blender. I'll close the factory where it's made.

CARLOS: ''When I designed that blender, when I hired the people in the factory, I expected they'd put out a decent product. I'm closing the factory. I'm canceling the patent!''
This is another inappropriate action, given Carlos's po-

sition, but it is included as an illustration of Level Five in action.

SEXY SHEILA

MALE CO-WORKER (RANDY) (in front of several employees): "Hey, Sam, I won the lotto. I get to spend the afternoon making it with Sheila in the boardroom."

Sheila does the Four F'S:

1. FORGIVE.
2. FEELING fear. Why? What's the fantasy?
3. FANTASY—I'm anyone's property to exploit sexually.
4. FANTASTIC FANTASY—Yeah, right. I'm just a hunk of meat—but *he* might want to think about it first.

SHEILA: "I'm not sure the boardroom is available. The Army or Navy or somebody's borrowing it for an official hearing . . . something about sexual harassment charges. . . . Someone said the media's here, too."

CATHERINE AND HER COUSIN

ARCHIE: (Rant, rave, rave, rant. Catherine waits patiently for him to address a situation close to home before she neutralizes.) "And I'm movin' to a place where I don't have to pay property taxes . . . a place where I don't have to fund other people's kids in school [Catherine has two school-age kids.] Why should I have to pay for your children to get an education? I've already paid for mine."

Catherine does the Four F'S:

1. FORGIVE (not easy).
2. FEELING anger, or rather its flip side, fear. What is the fantasy?
3. FANTASY—His needs are important and matter, and my kids' needs don't. Stick with it; what is he really saying? My kids are not worth his taxes to educate.
4. FANTASTIC FANTASY—My kids, *all* kids aren't worth educating.

CATHERINE: "You know, Archie, you're absolutely right! I've supported these spoiled brats long enough. It's high time they got jobs and began supporting themselves. I'll pull them outta school this week. That'll be two less in the school system. Maybe you and I can convince the education department to stop public education after the eighth grade. Think about it, Archie, this is an idea whose time has come."

As mentioned before, Archie needs more help than Catherine can give him. He needs professional counseling. Knowing Archie's terror of death and disability, Catherine could probably execute an awesome Level Five on that subject. However, in view of the large amount of negative energy that Archie attacks with, it might prove almost fatal for Archie if she reversed all of it. She might successfully neutralize current and future manipulations, but she would feel guilty anyway if he keeled over with a heart attack. So Catherine chooses to limit the range of Level Five subjects that she uses. She chooses, quite simply, to follow the Golden Rule.

Besides, as Catherine moves comfortably up and down the five levels, Archie's manipulative behavior begins to change. Catherine no longer provides the power he needs to feel better. She no longer plays the game using his rules. She doesn't counterattack or get emotional as she used to.

She provides no fuel for Archie's fire. Catherine ceases to be a victim.

And while Archie doesn't come around as much any more (to Catherine's relief), he tries to be on his better behavior when he does.

The five levels presented here can be viewed as a system to help you defend yourself against manipulation. Just like the soft martial artist, you can defend yourself without counterattacking.

In addition, we, the authors, discovered that by using this system, you can actually *modify* the behavior of some of the manipulators toward you—especially those whom you encounter on a regular basis in your life. In continuing relationships, the manipulative people *learn* that they cannot sap your strength, they cannot engage you in an emotional argument. Attempts to control you, amazingly, seem to backfire. The manipulators get tired of being slimed by their own negative energy. And they begin to approach you in a more respectful and reasonable fashion.

CHAPTER 10

Manipulating Ourselves

When a person tries to manipulate us through the use of guilt and fear, we can recognize this and label it. We know where we stand. This person wants some of our power, and we can protect ourselves accordingly without counterattacking. But what if no one appears to be manipulating us? And we are still beaten up with fear and guilt? Maybe we are forcing ourselves through our own guilt to do something we don't want to do. Maybe we are afraid of things that are only imaginary. Self-imposed guilt and self-imposed fear are powerful ghost manipulations from earlier periods in our lives that come forward to haunt us now.

MANIPULATING OURSELVES THROUGH GUILT

In the following illustrations, there is no manipulator laying a guilt trip. The guilt is totally self-imposed. This is not to say that any garden-variety manipulator won't be able to make use of this guilt in a big way once he or she suspects any vulnerable areas. When we can identify our own self-imposed guilt, we can work on letting it go. Heaven knows, we have so much guilt coming at us from every direction that it's refreshing to be able to release some of the excess baggage.

In the following examples, you may be able to identify with the guilt. On the other hand, you may have a high guilt threshold and feel not one twinge of it. Good for you!

1. You meet a friend for lunch. You both order the daily special. It's a massive amount of food. You can only eat about half of your lunch. You can't take the leftovers back to the office; the fridge is broken. You feel awful leaving all that food on your plate. You feel guilty. Why?

2. It's been over a month since you phoned your mom. Now you realize she and Dad have probably taken off for several weeks on a vacation. No one answers the phone. You feel awful. Why?

3. You, your husband, and your three kids are just finishing up one of the worst years you've ever been through, with illness, stress, and problems galore. The holiday season is fast approaching. Traditionally, all the relatives meet at your house for the festivities. You usually give the neighborhood party as well. This year all you want to do is cancel the holidays, forget decorating, forget entertaining, and instead pack up your family and go out of town. Yet you can't even bear mentioning the idea. Why?

4. You are on a hiking trail up in the mountains. You can walk for several miles before meeting someone else along the way. You look down. You spot a twenty dollar bill on the path. There is not a soul in sight. Not even an official ranger station nearby. Finding the owner would be hopeless. Keeping the money makes you uncomfortable. Why?

5. Your child gets into mischief at school. The penalties

are clear. He pays the price, repents, and wants to get on with his life. You, on the other hand, feel just terrible. Why?

6. You've invited company over for dinner on Saturday. You are so far behind in your own life that you need to spend Saturday playing catch-up, not in the kitchen fixing an elegant dinner. You remember that your local grocery store now has a bakery and salad and soup bar where the finest clam chowder you've ever tasted resides. You go to the grocery store, buy four quarts of the chowder, get fresh French bread, salad stuff, and a fancy dessert. You dump the clam chowder into your crockpot. The company raves over your "homemade chowder" and asks for the recipe. You clam up and feel uncomfortable. Why?

7. The company president calls you in. You've been selected to represent the company at the International Quokka Watchers Convention to be held in Australia. All expenses paid. All your life you've dreamt of going to Australia. But you realize you can't afford to take your spouse and kids to the Land Down Under. You go belly-up. Why?

8. You've got an important meeting at work. Yet your son has an important cross-country track meet the same time that afternoon. He's told you that he wouldn't even know if you were there or not. You still feel guilty. Why?

9. You are at your favorite department store. On the clearance rack you spot an elegant cocktail dress in size six. You can't imagine why no one has bought it. Although you haven't been a size six since you were six, wonders of wonders, it fits beautifully. It's been marked down from $100 to $50, then had another 50 percent taken off, so it's now $25. You have a coupon

for 50 percent off any clearance item. You now have a gorgeous dress for $12.50. In fact, it's the prettiest dress you have in your closet. Which is where it stays and stays and stays. Why won't you wear it?

10. You get an A in a class you're taking. While you know you should be thrilled with the A, you are disappointed that it is a low A. You get your next exam paper back. You scored 95 percent. You feel miserable because it's not 100 percent. Why?

Now, not one, not one, person in the above examples has made you feel guilty. Except yourself. In the leftover lunch example, the waiter didn't even inquire whether anything was wrong with the lunch. And the friend didn't ask if you were off your feed lately. The topic never came up. You just sat there looking at all that food going to waste and feeling miserably guilty. Were you asked to clean your plate as a child? Are you concerned about the hungry people in the world? No one has made you take on that responsibility. You paid for the lunch, you ate what you could, and you'll now go back to work. There is no point making yourself sick or adding an extra inch to your waistline. Next time you eat there, you'll ask them how large the portions are. Maybe order a salad instead.

In the second instance, Mom never seems hurt when you don't call, even for weeks or months. She's busy living her own life. And you'll probably get a postcard from Lake Tahoe. She'd be upset if she thought you felt guilty for not phoning.

Canceling the holidays or rather celebrating them away from home is a radical departure for you and the family. But what if, just what if, the whole family would love to go to the beach for the holidays, say, "Thank the Lord, we made it through this difficult year," and treat themselves to a long-deserved break from the stress. Traditions and routines can bind us in ways that allow spontaneity to fly right up the chimney. You might be surprised just how enthusiastically the family will react. And it won't kill the neighbors to wait till the dust settles before you throw a party.

Finding the money on the path was a bit of a surprise. Chances are strong that the hiker that lost it won't be back this way before another hiker comes along, spots it, and picks it up. If you should stumble upon a park ranger, you could tell him you found it and give him your number. Otherwise, how are you going to advertise? "Found a twenty dollar bill. Anyone missing a twenty dollar bill, please call me at. . . ." You'll never receive so many phone calls in your life.

Someone once said, "You cannot even define guilt until you are a parent." When your child gets into trouble, you feel the crushing weight of having dropped the ball, literally, like a bowling ball onto your bare foot. You can tell yourself: Give him the freedom to learn, to fail and to grow. Then, like most parents, you'll try to kill yourself with guilt when the child occasionally fails. In this case, the school was neutral. The student paid the consequences. No one thought the worst of the child. He was forgiven. But the parent often cannot create self-forgiveness. Parents tend to integrate their children's behavior into their own self-expectations. All too often, the child becomes the model with which the parents pass judgment on *themselves*.

The clam chowder incident serves to illustrate, along with the cocktail dress incident, how we can feel undeserving of praise, real or potential, when we expend less energy or money than is expected of us by others.

The Australia trip would be a dream come true except for feeling guilty that you cannot take the family. And even if you didn't feel guilty, you'd probably end up feeling guilty for not feeling guilty! The family might be disappointed. But they will probably be thrilled that you get the chance to go.

The parent who feels guilty because he or she can't make the cross-country track meet has set up the unrealistic expectation of being present for every single one of his or her child's activities. The child has even gone so far to say that he won't be able to tell if the parent is there. The child isn't imposing the guilt. The parent is imposing it on parent.

And finally, when we feel guilty about not achieving something that we aimed for, perhaps we need to look and see if we didn't aim too high. What is a realistic expectation in this situation? An A is an A is an A. Why beat up on ourselves when we missed only one question? We feel we could have done better, and we feel guilty.

You can easily look around and see those people in your life who are constantly coming from a position of guilt. They usually speak with heavy doses of "I should have done . . ." Or "I should have said . . . ," and so on. You can imagine the guilt oozing from their pores. Often you can see the guilt in their posture, a slight stoop, with body language that says, "I'm sorry. I don't deserve nice things happening to me."

Whom do you know who is always feeling guilty for spending too much money? For not taking better care of his or her elderly parents? For not coming to church or synagogue regularly? For not exercising more, eating less, or quitting a bad habit?

Every time you feel guilty for doing or not doing something, ask yourself if it is self-imposed, or is there a manipulator trying to make you feel crummy? You might be surprised just how often you are controlled by the ghost manipulators of your past.

MANIPULATING OURSELVES THROUGH FEAR

The following example happened to a friend and illustrates how our own fears can dictate our responses, however reasonable or unreasonable they may be:

This friend, an elderly lady, was driving her older car home from the store alone, at rush hour. She was going no place fast on the on ramp to Interstate 80. She caught movement out of the corner of her eye. Suddenly a man's face was peering in through the open window. "Your keys." His tone was demanding. "Your keys, lady," he repeated louder. A thousand thoughts raced through the woman's mind. Why would he want to steal her old car? Why was this happening to her? Her eyes shifted from his face. In his hand was a set of keys. "You left these in the trunk of your car, lady."

When we look at how we manipulate ourselves through fear, it is also interesting to examine those areas where we get angry. Many times anger is just the flip side of fear. Anger is a form of attack. It comes up when the body's adrenaline kicks in with the proverbial flight-or-fight mechanism. Where there is openness, love, communication, and peace, there is no anger. Anger generally comes from fear. We'll go one step further to state that many times fear generates anger, and anger can crystallize into hatred. Fear, anger, hatred. None of them is a pleasant emotion.

When we look at what makes people angry, we can often identify the underlying fear. In each of the following illustrations, see if you can identify what the basic fear is.

1. Your daughter's grades the first term in college are abysmal. You scraped and saved to send her to the university. She is a bright young adult, capable of getting great grades. You get angry. Why?

2. Your elderly father phones and asks you for the eleventh time today if you know who stole his wallet. No one stole his wallet. He just keeps misplacing it. You get angry. Why?

3. Your son has a habit of leaving his tricycle parked behind the car in the driveway. You have repeatedly told him not to leave it there. You back out and run over it. You get angry. Why?

4. Your wife or husband loves to shop. He or she never comes home empty-handed. He or she is generous to a fault, buying neat clothes and gifts for you and the kids, and it seems, everyone else. Each month at bill-paying time it's a nightmare. You both make the same amount of money, but between you, it's never enough. Today your spouse walks in with an armload of purchases. You get angry. Why?

5. Your cat is a well-behaved and good-natured animal, except toward those people in your life you desperately want to impress and make feel welcome in your home, for example, your boss, your mother-in-law, your parish priest. When these people come over, Fluffy acts like a pit bull. For a while there, you locked the cat in the bathroom. But Fluffy gave a new definition to the word "caterwauling." Finally, you decide to let Fluffy have one more chance. During dinner, the cat leaps onto the table and grabs a piece of chicken off your boss's wife's plate. When she says gently, "No, no, kitty, that's mine," Fluffy hisses and bites her. You get angry. (At your cat, not the boss's wife.) Why?

6. Your child comes home in tears, his lip cut, his eye a real shiner. He just got roughed up by a couple of bullies down the street. Your child feels manipulated and you get angry. Why?

7. Your daughter is barely sixteen. You tell her she can go to a certain party if a parent is present in the house and her curfew is midnight. You receive a call at 11:45: Her car won't start. You go to the party house to get her. You discover that no parent is chaperoning. You get angry. Why?

8. You've been up all night cramming for an exam. You've had to memorize the entire history of civilization down to dates and leaders. You've lived off coffee and adrenaline for the past forty some hours. You get to class. The teacher comes in and apologizes. He forgot to bring the exam. It'll be postponed until Monday. You get angry. Why?

9. You've moved. You go to a new doctor. You tell him that you take this prescription for a special ailment and that it works. He has your records from your former trusted physician. This new doctor looks at you and says, "I don't prescribe this. I use Brand Y instead. I've found it to be far superior." You tell him you're allergic to Brand Y and that's why you want the other prescription. He tells you that nobody is allergic to Brand Y. You get angry. Why?

10. You've been looking long and hard for a part-time job, having been out of the work force for eight years, raising kids. You go for an interview at an insurance company. The young female manager looks you up and down and says, "I don't know how I'd feel being the supervisor of someone old enough to be my mother." You get angry. Why?

What are the fear or fears fueling each of the above individuals' anger? In these exact same instances, you as an individual might not feel any anger, you might not feel any fear, but suppose the characters above did. Why are they feeling anger, and not recognizing their fears? Is it easier to experience anger than to get in touch with fear?

Could you, as the parent, be fearful that your daughter will flunk out of the university and, therefore, out of the life you may wish for her?

Do you fear that your parent might be getting something more serious than a case of forgetfulness? Maybe becoming dependent upon other people for care? For possible institutionalization and the effort and money that might require?

Could you, who ran over the trike, fear that you could hit somebody, not something? Instead, it's easier to be angry over the trouble and expense of getting another tricycle or explaining to the child why he can't ride the thing anymore.

Are you afraid that unless you can keep on top of the bills, you quite simply won't have enough money one month to make the mortgage payment? Is each of you worried about really communicating with the other?

Your boss just might equate the cat's behavior with some unconscious feelings that you may have, which is what you fear. Also, what if the cat bite gets infected? Does your homeowner's policy cover that? And finally, the boss might just feel that any person who cannot control an animal any better than this is in no position to be supervising other people.

The child has his first tangle with the neighborhood bullies. He arrives home in tatters. Do you now fear the bullies and what they can continue to do to your child? Does Dad fear tattling on the bullies because that may only bring further fights?

Do you worry about losing control over your teenage daughter or having someone taking advantage of her? She went to an unsupervised party.

In the case of the exam, do you worry that you can't memorize that stuff all over again without putting in another day and a half? "It just isn't fair." Life isn't fair. Or rather, at times, it does not appear that way. This in itself is fearful. Like, who is in control? We can fear change, randomness, and chaos. Confronted with "Life isn't fair," we often begin to doubt all kinds of things—life, death, order in the universe. "Hello, isn't someone minding the store?"

In the case of the doctor, you have just spent the time, money, and effort to meet this new M.D. You also know what you want and what you don't want. Yet, the doctor, not you, has the power of the pen to write that prescription. You now have to start all over again, with the fear that maybe the next doctor will respond the same way. And you'll never get that prescription, and your fungus will spread all over your body, and before long you'll turn into a giant mushroom.

To the aged and decrepit thirty-seven-year-old you, the manager's quip cut to the quick. Is this how you're viewed? Somebody's mother? Oh, well, just a few short years till Social Security. Forget the part-time job. Too old!

We can and do manipulate ourselves with fear. Just as we do with guilt. It can be interesting to look at those people close to you and see whether guilt or fear or both run their lives. Not only the superimposed guilt or superimposed fear of the manipulator, but also the internal, self-imposed fear and guilt with which they manipulate themselves.

One friend we have loves going to Southern California. She flies down, rents a convertible, and takes to the freeways like tulips to spring. She changes lanes, and if she gets in the wrong one, she goes on to the next exit and doubles back around in the right direction. Blond hair streaming behind her, radio blasting, she heads off for lunch at Laguna Beach, then shopping at Newport Beach and back to Disneyland for an evening of rides.

Another friend of ours is terrified of flying anyplace, especially Southern California. Besides the plane possibly crashing, she is scared of earthquakes, mud slides, fires, and riots. Once she gets there, she won't drive. She relies on friends or local transportation. She needs tranquilizers to ride with anyone on the freeways. The last time she went to Disneyland, it took two attendants almost ten minutes to pry her fingers off the safety bar on the bobsled ride at the Matterhorn.

Whom do you know who is always worried about losing his job? Or conversely, whom do you know who feels secure in her job and confident that if she should lose this one, another even better job will be available?

Whom do you know who can never have enough material possessions? Who is driven by a fear of lack or loss? Or do you know someone who is almost eccentric in his or her total disinterest in material things?

Whom do you know who protects his or her children so much they are almost smothered? Conversely, you may know parents who let their children do just about anything as long as it's legal.

Do you know others who are always afraid that their spouses may cheat on them? Jealously is a powerful fear. Or conversely, others who never give that notion a second thought?

How about the person who worries endlessly about her health? That's fear. Like the tombstone above the ninety-nine-year-old hypochondriac who died: "See, I said I was sick.'' Or consider the other person who avoids doctors, never takes care of herself, and spends about five minutes a year considering her health.

The list could go on and on. When we can recognize our own self-imposed fears, we are not as easily manipulated by ourselves into doing strange things. Nor are we as easily manipulated by others. Interestingly enough, the garden-variety manipulator seems to have the ability to zero in on our most vulnerable areas, using the weapon of fear. Those areas where we, ourselves, feel the most fear. To know is to be forewarned and forearmed. By knowing ourselves better, we can protect ourselves against those individuals who attempt to control us in order to feel better about themselves.

THE DYSFUNCTIONAL FICTIONAL FAMILY

Instead of looking at a true case history, let's invent a totally fictional family, the members of which are having a bad week involving the manipulations in their life—not abuse, but ten times their share of everyday manipulations in every sector, along with no small amount of self-imposed guilt and fear. Let's see how they go about neutralizing it.

Mom is divorced from Dad. Mom has a Boyfriend. Dad has remarried; we'll name his new wife New Wife. Mom works full-time at XYZ Corporation downtown. Mom lives with her two children, Son (twelve years old) and Daughter (sixteen years old). They are renting a small house with a lease option to buy. They drive an old car. Son has a newspaper route and Daughter works part-time at a jazz hangout/coffeehouse located near the university campus. They have an indoor housecat named Nice Kitty. Currently, there is excellent communication among everyone. Mom, Son, and

Daughter are pretty happy, actually. Hope abounds, and life is worth living.

Now, how can we make their lives a nightmare of manipulation? Let's see where we can introduce control—control over how they think, feel, and behave—to cause them discomfort. Let's throw in some heavy doses of guilt and fear, the weapons of the manipulator. The family will do an adequate job of supplying their own self-imposed fear and guilt as well.

Now, which areas of their lives will be affected? Since we are going for broke, how about *everywhere?* Family, job, social, church, as well as random acts. Random acts, by the way, are distributed statistically along a normal bell curve. In this case, the fictional family will receive its full 5 percent of a lifetime, all at once, now.

Monday morning and it's raining. Mom receives a phone call from ex-husband Dad. He informs her that he'll be late with the child support check this month because New Wife has to put money down for her orthodontics. How late? About two weeks. Not good news.

The office is switching computer systems, and Mom has just been informed that she will have to work late all this week, since that is the only time the systems programmer is available. While this creates a problem, since Daughter needs the car in the evenings, at least the overtime will help with the money supply. Son informed her this morning that his coach insists on first-class athletic shoes. The cost? $120.

Tuesday evening, Mom drags home late to find three phone messages. She returns them. The first is her minister trying to talk her into teaching Sunday school. Yet, both her kids have been attending a different church lately. The second message is from her grandmother in Arizona. She is coming to visit and will be arriving in two days. The third is from the neighbor down the street. Pretty please could Mom take care of their indoor cat while they are on vacation? They can't bear the thought of putting Strange Pussy in the boarding parlor.

Wednesday, Mom notices that the house next door, which has been vacant, is now rented. Her new neighbors include a dozen College Kids. They christen their new lodging with a loud party that goes on all night. Cars rev, bottles break, and stereos boom. It's still raining. Lots of rain. So, consistent with Murphy's Law, the water pump goes out in the car and the car ends up at the mechanic. Unfortunately, the car is so old that the mechanic has to order the repair part from Sacramento. The car is out of commission for the rest of the week.

Daughter brings home her new boyfriend. Not the clean-shaven youth Mom is used to seeing. No one except Daughter would want to be caught in an alley with this guy. Mom complains to Daughter. Daughter says, "But he's really nice. You can't judge him just because of the way he looks." Mom's Boyfriend jumps into the fracas, putting his foot squarely down, pretending to be Dad, and alienates both Son and Daughter.

Strange Pussy, the neighbor's cat, begins attacking Nice Kitty. Nice Kitty goes crazy and starts tearing her fur out. Nice Vet puts Nice Kitty on tranquilizers.

Thursday, Mom gets a call at work from Son. The good news? He'll be on the evening news. The bad news? He's been suspended for two days for going AWOL from middle school and marching with a bunch of students on the state offices to protest the budget cuts to the school district. It is still raining. The seven-year drought has been broken, with three years' worth of rain so far.

Late Thursday evening, Granny arrives. She has the unnerving habit of chain smoking and leaving the cigarettes hanging off the edge of the kitchen counter, or dangling in ashtrays or saucers. Mom is afraid Granny is going to burn the house down, but then she realizes that the rain would probably put out any fire.

Daughter announces that the youth group at her new church is sending the youth to a sister church in Guatemala to build a clinic by the dump. They'll go over spring break, and it will only cost $1,000 a person.

Now, what else can we do to make this gang's life even more miserable?

Friday, Son and Daughter go to stay at Dad's and New Wife's house. They overhear New Wife complaining about the child support payment. New Wife asks, since she stays home, why not take custody of the kids and save having to pay the support altogether? Son and Daughter vow to tell Mom when they get home Saturday.

On Saturday, Mom gets a call from her bosses at the XYZ Corporation. The Turkey River is overflowing its banks. She needs to come to the office and "rescue" her files, computer, etc., so they won't be damaged by the floodwaters.

When Mom and Boyfriend arrive, they find Son and Daughter perched precariously close to the raging river. They are hoisting sandbags along with half the town. Son and Daughter inform Mom of New Wife's idea for creative financing.

Sunday morning, the telephone rings. The college crowd from next door is calling to complain that Son did not have the paper on the porch by 5:30 A.M. Mom explains that the papers don't need to be delivered until 6:30 A.M. Irate College Kid informs Mom that he is calling the circulation manager anyway.

Mom informs the minister that she can't teach Sunday school, no matter what happens to her soul. She asks the minister if he does exorcisms. Minister informs her that perhaps she may wish to consider attending a different church.

Now, what Mom would like to do is take the last few dollars in her checking account and buy a one-way ticket to the Bahamas. However, she is a responsible parent and will not do this. Mom looks at the various situations and realizes that her life is rapidly going out of control.

What would you recommend that Mom do? Perhaps take the whole picture and break it down into manageable pieces? Then look for where the manipulation, however subconscious it may be, appears. Next, she could look at which buttons are being pushed by fear and guilt.

Fear first. What are the family's fears? That New Wife may somehow get custody? That Mom and Boyfriend will marry and add a new dynamic to the family? That the College Kids next door will get Son fired from his paper route? That the College Kids next door will do something dreadful to them or their house? That Daughter will elope with New Boyfriend, who makes a social statement by his appearance? That Daughter will actually raise enough money to go with the church to Guatemala and never be heard from again? That Son's suspension will label him as a trouble-maker and his grades will plummet? That Mom won't have the money to keep the old car going much longer, let alone enough money to pay an attorney in a custody battle? That Granny will set the house on fire? That Nice Kitty will become addicted to tranquilizers? That Mom will go straight to Hell for not teaching Sunday school?

How about guilt? Where does Mom feel the guilt? She must be an awful mom to comment on her daughter's boyfriend. She must be an awful mom to have a son suspended from school. She must be a terrible mom to tell her son he can't have the $120 for new shoes. She'll feel guilty if she makes Granny smoke outside. She feels guilty for wanting to strangle Strange Pussy. She even feels guilty for entertaining thoughts of calling the police the next time College Kids throw a wild party. She feels guilty for feeling angry at her boss, now that her living room looks like her office, complete with computers, files, etc. At least she has a job.

Mom calls a family meeting. Mom's Boyfriend is invited also. Granny is down at the clubs gambling. Mom explains that there is a whole lot of manipulation going on. She also discusses guilt and fear and asks her children what they are feeling in each of the various situations. Daughter mentions that she feels crummy that Mom hates New Boyfriend. Daughter also states that she's upset with Mom's Boyfriend pretending he's Dad. And she's really uptight that New Wife is talking about custody. She wants to go to Guatemala with the church youth group.

Son is unhappy because someone next door called the newspaper and complained. He also feels crummy that he can't get the $120 shoes his coach strongly recommends. He regrets marching on the state offices to protest the school budget cuts, having gotten hyped up in the spirit of the moment. He's worried about his zoned-out cat and Granny burning the house down. And he's afraid it will never stop raining.

Mom feels free to share how she feels guilty and afraid when life seemingly goes out of control. Mom asks for suggestions in dealing with the various issues. And asks everyone to bear in mind that there are at least four possible ways of handling each issue, short of violence:

Ignoring the situation (Level One).

Continuing polite behavior while ignoring the manipulation (Level Two).

Clarifying to see if a manipulation is really a manipula-

tion and allowing for appropriate behavior (Level Three).
Calling in an outside party, real or fictitious (Level Four).

1. No one can stop the rain. It cannot rain more than
   another thirty-three days, they all reason. God prom-
   ised never again to destroy the earth by flood. Maybe
   by fire, though, if Granny can't get remember to ex-
   tinguish her smokes. (Level One)
2. Granny is leaving for home tomorrow. Before Granny
   returns, the family will instigate a nonsmoking policy
   at home. If Granny wants to smoke, she can smoke
   outside. (Level Three)
3. Someone will call the veterinarian to be assured that
   Nice Kitty won't get addicted to the tranquilizers. And
   it's only a few more days till the neighbor gets back
   and takes Strange Pussy home. (Level Three)
4. Mom will talk to each of the neighbors nearby to see
   what their reactions to the College Kids are. If they
   feel threatened, Mom will find out who owns the rental
   house and phone them, under the assumption that the
   owner doesn't want his or her house destroyed either.
   (Level Four)
5. Mom will talk to Dad privately at work, away from New
   Wife, and see if, in fact, there is any reason to be concerned over the custody comments. Dad may be late in
   child support payments, but otherwise they are on reasonable terms with each other. If Dad assures Mom that
   no way is he going to promote New Wife's agenda, then
   they can all rest more comfortably. If on the other hand,
   Dad thinks this is an idea whose time has come, then
   Mom will be prepared to bring in outside legal expertise. If she cannot afford an attorney, then she would
   probably qualify for legal assistance through several
   programs run by the country. (Levels Three and Four)

6. Mom will phone the principal at the school. It is questionable just how hard some of the teachers tried to prevent the march. Why not have the kids who marched write letters to the legislators instead? She will get assurance in any respect that Son will not be unjustly penalized for his actions. (Level Three)

7. Mom's Boyfriend volunteers that he is sorry for acting like Dad. He doesn't have a clue how to relate to teenagers. He is crazy about Mom. He apologizes. He tells the kids frankly that marriage might be a possibility but that it's down the road. Heck, the kids might even be out of the nest by then. (Level Three)

8. Mom agrees that Daughter can go to Guatemala, provided she raises half the money herself. Mom isn't in a position to give her the full $1,000. Mom suggests she might tag along with Son and Daughter to their church. Her own minister isn't all that happy with her at the moment. (Levels Two and Three)

9. Mom asks Son if he knows someone on the team who has outgrown his shoes. If so, maybe Son could buy them at a large discount. Or, he could try the second-hand athletic store. Soon, when his feet are another size bigger, hopefully finances will be better and Mom can get him a new pair. (Level Two)

10. Mom apologizes to Daughter for her negative comments about the boyfriend. "I'm sure if you like him, he's super. Should make a great son-in-law." Daughter responds with "I'm thinking about dumping him anyway." This is fiction; what more can we say? (Level Three)

Can you see how our family above manages by using a combination of Levels One through Four? Ignoring; continuing polite behavior while ignoring the manipulation; ascertaining whether there is manipulation or not, and allowing for appropriate behavior; calling in an outside party if necessary to witness (verify) the manipulation—they used them all. Sorting out what they could do something about was a start. By examining the underlying guilt and fear, they identified more quickly the control issues involved. And set about making things better for all of them.

And making things better for all of us is what this book is about. We can learn to avoid counterattacking. We can improve communication. We can be strong and vulnerable both at the same time. We can let go of some of our own fear and guilt and feel more comfortable. We can let go of some of the wrongs and hurts we nurse from our past and feel ever so much freer.

We can teach ourselves not to hurt one another. We can teach ourselves other ways than verbal violence to handle verbal conflict. We can teach ourselves some basic principles that promote peace.

We *can* protect ourselves.

CHAPTER 11

Conclusion

Life Is More Than Just Dealing With Manipulation

Manipulation involves power and control. The primary weapons of the manipulator are *guilt* and *fear*. It's those elements of discomfort from fear and guilt that propel normal interaction with others into the realm of manipulation.

The manipulators are acting out of insecurity. They are unsure of who they are and what their position is. They are less in control of their own lives than you are. If they can find a way to control you, they feel they are in control of their lives. When they can make you feel rotten, and they've taken you down a few pegs, that person can say, "Well, then I must be okay."

Manipulation is addictive. Manipulating is so addictive that some people will actually maneuver themselves into jobs where they will elevate themselves to a certain level and resist promotions so that they can continue to manipulate and control those individuals below them.

Manipulation is a dare or a threat. I dare you to play my game—so I dare you to call me hostile. I dare you to call me a manipulator. "I'm going to take my ball and go home if you do that." Power and control. If you take the dare, you lose. You can never beat a manipulator at his or her game by saying, "Hey, you're manipulating me." You can't do it; it won't work, because the manipulator will always say, "What are you talking about . . . doing what?"

Let's say someone has tried to hit you. If you play by their rules, they've got you. They want you to counterattack. If you choose to do this at this point, you may as well say, "Here, you take my Colt 45, I'll just use this water pistol." It is up to you to create a whole new set of rules. Rules that are unpredictable. The manipulators will realize either consciously or subconsciously that their manipulation of you is not working. You are patterning their behavior, not vice versa.

So how do you defend yourself and not counterattack? The metaphor of choice for the purposes of this book has been the soft (unarmed) martial arts. Here the power of the attacker flows through you and back onto the attacker. The energy of the attacker is used against him or her.

We are not talking about passivity. Here, take this collar and put it around my neck. No! Likewise, we are not talking about aggression, where you counterattack and try to control the manipulator. Instead, you practice an alert assertiveness that says, in effect, I am the one mentally, emotionally, and physically in control of myself, not you. I will continue to live my life as I choose and to protect myself while doing minimal damage to you, my opponent. With successful neutralization, there is no loss of your personal power or energy to the other person. We are attempting to neutralize the manipulation and restore communication, not kill the manipulator.

To review, let's look at the following illustrations of the five levels:

Level One: A sixteen-year-old girl went to buy a battery-pack screwdriver for her dad for his birthday. She went to a large discount store. Most of the tools were kept in a glass case near the back of the store. A clerk standing by the case was obviously being reprimanded by her supervisor. After the supervisor left, the teenager told the store clerk she wanted to buy a particular screwdriver. The price was a little over twenty dollars. The clerk handed it to her, then announced in a loud voice, "I'll have to walk you to the checkout counter." The teen continued walking, carrying the bulky screwdriver. The clerk, hot on her heels, kept calling out, "I'll have to walk you to the checkout counter." The teenager ignored her and continued walking toward the checkout counter. The clerk still continued to call out. The remark, unheard and ignored by the teenager, failed to make its mark. The clerk was attempting to bait her into an argument. First of all, the battery-pack screwdriver was hardly a piece of gold jewelry. Secondly, it was bulky and hard to hide on your person. And finally, most teenage girls are not into stealing screwdrivers. And yet the implication was obvious: that the teenager could not be trusted and might try to shoplift the screwdriver. Arguing would accomplish nothing. "Why do you have to walk me to the checkout counter?" "Store policy." "Well, I'm certainly not planning on stealing the screwdriver." "Store policy. If you want, you go ahead and pay for it and I'll deliver it to the checkout counter." Ad nauseam. More was accomplished by the teenager informing her parents, who talked directly to the store manager. No, it was not store policy. Yes, teenagers have a great deal of discretionary income, and yes, the store would like them to spend some of it there.

Level Two: A man starts to enter a grocery store. He is cornered by a lady with a clipboard. "Are you a registered voter?" "Yes," he replies. The lady continues, "Well, we are collecting signatures for a petition to outlaw any reference to Valentine's Day." The man replies, "You're a hearty soul to be standing here in fifteen-degree weather," smiles warmly, and walks into the grocery store.

Level Three: A teenage boy asks his dad if he can go skiing the next Saturday. His dad replies, "Sure, if the weather is reasonable and you've got enough money saved up." The son sulkily says, "Jeez, Dad, you never let me do anything! Some father *you* are." The father says, "I don't want you driving up on the pass if you'll need to chain up or if a storm warning is in effect." The son argues, "But I can learn how to put chains on, and besides no one knows what the weather will be like." The father says, "Look, it makes me feel guilty in advance when someone wants me to promise something I may not be able to deliver. Let's look at the weather closer to the weekend."

Level Four: A woman calls the billing office at her doctor's office because she has just received a nasty late notice from them. She doesn't understand why. The doctor's office billed her insurance company, and the woman even received a form from the insurance company indicating that the bill was paid. The billing clerk is belligerent and states that no payment has been received. The woman says she has a copy showing that the insurance company paid them directly. The billing clerk informs her that unless payment is made immediately, the woman will be turned over to a collection agent. The woman states, "Will you please repeat what you just said, slowly, so I can write it all down? I want to be absolutely certain I have your name and your statement correct."

Level Five: A policeman pulls a speeding motorist over. He asks to see the man's driver's license. The motorist starts mouthing off to the cop, sputtering and defensive as all get out. "I'll have you know I *pay your salary!*" he says. The cop replies, "I know, I've been looking for you—my paycheck hasn't arrived yet," as he hands him the speeding ticket.

The following paragraphs summarize how each level accomplishes the neutralizing of manipulation.

We saw with Level One how we ignore both the manipulator and the manipulation. If we came over to you and said, "Can we borrow this? . . . Uh, can we borrow this? . . . Uh, can we . . . Hello, are you there?" we are the ones with the problem. Even though we have every reason to believe that you can hear us (you did five minutes ago), our brain is going to think that all of a sudden your ears have stopped functioning. Likewise, when you ignore the manipulator completely, he or she is going to believe that *your* ears have stopped functioning. A sudden attack of deafness. That simple. Why do you do this? Because you are going to give the manipulators the opportunity to correct those obnoxious statements they just made. You are giving them a fair shot and a chance to begin to hear what they are actually saying. And a chance to correct it. We have seen how our characters used Level One, in the family, home, and at work, with the exception of Marcy and Her Mom (can't exactly use Level One over the telephone . . . "Uh, hello?"). Level One is also the level of choice for people who flip you off while driving, say rude comments in general in the grocery store, and so on. By acting as if you have not seen or heard the rudeness, you ensure the attack has not made its mark and that the energy returns to the sender. This is known as "deafing." The concept is "Hear no evil." The subtitle here is "I hear you knocking, but there's no one home."

With Level Two, "Speak no evil," you ignore the manipulation but pay attention to the manipulator. Following rant, rave, rave, rant: "Oh, hi, I didn't see you standing there." You are still going to give him or her a fair shot at repeating the comment, this time, hopefully, in a non-manipulative fashion. This is the manipulator's second shot, assuming you've used Level One first. "Hey, I'm going to be nice, and you are going to be nice." It works a surprisingly large number of times. This neutralizes the manipulation without hurting anyone. It's fine if the manipulator knows you are doing it. It is almost like saying, "Look, I know you just did a manipulation on me. But I'm going to be nice to you and give you the opportunity to stop doing that, and we can now go back to relating like before the manipulation. Instead of trying to hurt you or lay some big guilt trip on you, I'm just going to say, 'Hi, how are you?' . . . and you can think about what you just said." The subtitle for this level is "Have a nice day, anyway."

Level Three, often the first choice of those who are handy in the communications department, is "Permission" and seeks to ascertain whether or not a certain comment was indeed meant as a manipulation—without calling it that, of course. Level Three will clarify not only the other person's viewpoint but your own as well. A comment like "You know, my feelings get hurt when I get teased" will do one of two things. If the other person had no desire to control you, consciously or subconsciously, he or she will back off immediately. "I was just trying to include you as one of the guys." Or, "Hey, I wouldn't hurt you for the world." End of manipulation. However, if the other person denies the attempt, or starts to paint you into the crazy corner, or attacks with "Aren't *we* thin-skinned?" Or "Can't you take a joke?" you know you are in a manipulative situation. Often your only way out will be to agree and let it go. Responses such as "You may be right," or "That may be true," take the wind out of the sails of the would-be attacker, since you have neither fought nor given in.

By responding in the above manner, you make it perfectly clear that your attackers can manipulate all they please—by themselves thank you; you are not going to be involved in any way. You are too busy living your life to engage in this. The subtitle here is "I understand; I will not participate; I have other things I prefer to do now."

In short, by being pointlessly agreeable or stating how you feel using Level Three, your vulnerability allows for apology, reasonable explanation, or correction of the behavior. This is the ultimate test to determine whether or not you are being manipulated, intentionally or unintentionally.

Level Four, "Focused Attention," is also known as "Please wait while you embarrass yourself with your own words." With this level, you call attention in a bigger way to what is usually intentional intimidation. Using several four- or five-line scripts, you draw attention to the other person. Here it is important that other people, or at least one other person (real or fictitious), get involved in witnessing this manipulator or being informed of his or her behavior. For instance, you can call in an outside party: "Hey, Larry, please come over here. . . . Now, will you please repeat what you just said to me in front of Larry here?" Level Four can be used with mediation or outside counseling. Here you are holding up the behavior for another to see, and hopefully to help clarify. Marriage and family counseling helps people to see how they may be subconsciously trying to control other family members.

And finally, with Level Five, "Reversal," the manipulative energy, following the principles of the soft martial arts, returns to the sender, full circle, leaving the intended target unaffected. If this is handled correctly, the manipulator will receive back the exact degree of negative energy he or she tried to impose on you in the first place. You literally turn the energy around, in such a way that the sender punches himself out with his own fist. You have learned how to identify the fantasy inherent in nearly every manipulation and to magnify it, making the fantasy real in a way that the other person did not expect. In short, Level Five's subtitle is "If you think this fits me, let's see how it looks on you."

There is no big mystery about the five levels. No magic. All five concepts have been around for a long time. So has manipulation. Eve manipulated Adam into eating that apple, and things haven't gotten much better since!

Level One: Ignore.

Level Two: Turn the other cheek.

Level Three: Find out if in fact manipulation is occurring. If so, give permission, but without further involvement from you.

Level Four: Focus attention on the manipulator.

Level Five: Find the fantasy and make it real.

More than likely when you start using these neutralizing techniques, you'll help change the manipulators around you. *Seeing that they gain none of your power, or conversely that they receive back their own negative energy, will deter them from continued manipulation.* As you start using these neutralizing techniques, you'll also become more aware of what you are doing to other people, and how you manipulate yourself. It's very hard not to increase your awareness. This is therapeutic in itself, and lets you have a reality check on how your communication network is operating. Also, you can apply the techniques toward neutralizing the ghosts of your past—the manipulation ghosts from childhood on—and letting them go.

You saw how guilt and fear can be used as weapons by the garden-variety manipulator, and how easy it is to impose these on ourselves as well. We can beat up on ourselves both occasionally or continually through the use of guilt and/or fear.

One co-author lives in Nevada, where the sun shines thirteen months out of the year. The other lives in Oregon, where it is gray and rainy thirteen months out of the year. Yin and Yang. When friends and family visit the Nevada author, they comment on the warm summers and the sunny days spent upon the ski slopes in winter. Blue skies and crystal Tahoe beckon both winter and summer. There is no lack of entertainment—shows, gaming, balloon races, air races, ''Hot August Nights,'' etc. However, when friends and family visit the Oregon author the script is always the same. It goes like this:

VISITOR: ''Are the streetlights always on at noon?''

AUTHOR: ''Yes.''

VISITOR: (looking out the glass door leading to the backyard): ''Does it rain this hard all the time?''

AUTHOR: ''Yes.''

VISITOR: ''Did you know that the concrete on your patio is covered with green goop?''

AUTHOR: ''Yes.''

VISITOR: ''And get a load of that, you have mushrooms, lots of them, growing on your picnic table.''

AUTHOR: ''Yes.''

VISITOR: ''Oh, gross, hey, take a look at that. . . . What's *that thing?*''

AUTHOR: ''It's a slug. Garden-variety. A banana slug, actually.''

VISITOR: ''That thing's big enough to eat my cat! Get a load of the trail of slime behind it! Oh, yuck!''

AUTHOR: ''Actually, the slug is what the residents of Oregon use for entertainment. Here, take this saltshaker. You'll have to take the lid off; the holes are stopped up. And sprinkle the slug with salt. You won't believe your eyes—what happens, that is.''

VISITOR: ''Hey, you're puttin' me on.''

AUTHOR: "No. Actually, each September we have a festival and parade here. They pick the ugliest woman in town. She's crowned the Slug Queen, and she gets to ride on a float and lead the parade."

VISITOR: "Nawww...."

AUTHOR: "Yep, half the town's in the parade. The other half stands on the sidewalks under their umbrellas."

VISITOR: "Hey, that's kind of sick, isn't it?"

AUTHOR: "I'm just telling you like it is. Why, just last week, our son made ten dollars sucking a slug at school!"

VISITOR: "I know we just barely arrived and we had planned to stay until Thursday, but I think we'd better head back to Southern California this afternoon. I, uh, just remembered . . . I forgot to turn off the iron."

The Oregon author then feels more than her share of self-imposed guilt. No longer can she show people the good times as she did when they came to visit her in Nevada. Now that she's living in Oregon, what they see is what they get. They don't stay long. She feels personally responsible for the weather, the fungi, the moss, the slugs, the gray, and the rain.

Manipulation is not necessarily a one-on-one situation. Manipulation can be rampant every place. From the television news to advertising and more. It can become a group activity. Not limited to the family, office, social setting, synagogue, or church. It can take on larger and more definite proportions. Anytime you see the line drawn in the sand between "we" and "they," you need to pay attention. Anytime a leader of a group emerges and attempts to claim superiority over another group, take a look at where he or she is coming from. Is power and control involved? Usually. Is manipulation involved? Are fear and guilt being used to control how others think, feel, and behave?

Let's pick a group of people. Call them the People

Against Computer Users, PAC-U for short. This group of people has a leader, call him Mr. Packman. Now, in order for him to generate a following in his manipulative attempt to suppress the computer users of America, he will need to use, what? Fear and guilt. So let's look at how he can and will use fear and guilt. Look at the ghostly yet tangible aspects of those two emotions. Fear? Well, for one thing, let's look at health, politics, religion, and money. Computer users suffer ill health sometimes. Their eyes blur, their elbows swell, and their wrists seize up. How many thousands of dollars of taxpayers' money, your money, goes into treatment for these computer users? How many jobs are lost by computer-driven factory programs? Not to mention the lost jobs when we import (gasp) foreign computers and their parts. It is downright unAmerican, it is. As for morals, not one great holy book mentions computers. Heck, if God wanted us to have computers, he'd have given us computers along with Adam and Eve. Instead of the apple, maybe Eve would have talked Adam into giving her his password. Instead of the Apple, maybe Eve would have talked Adam out of his IBM. And none of this addresses just how addictive computer usage is. Why any teenage computer hacker will tell you that it bypasses drugs in its thrill. If fear itself weren't enough to get you to jump on the bandwagon, then how about guilt? You are personally responsible for all the world's problems if you don't stop the computer users in this world. You and you alone make the difference. Can you see how we get coerced? Manipulation gets played over and over again in all aspects of life.

LETTING GO

The philosophy of the soft martial arts lets us look at power and energy in any encounter in a different light. It focuses on flowing and defusing, or evading. It emphasizes changing the rules so that the energy of the attacker reverts *back* to the attacker and does not end up used against you. By being alert, but relaxed, you prove that you are the one in control—of yourself, your body, your mind, and your emotions. Where the oak might break in the storm, the willow bends. In the chapter on Level Three, we stated that strength though vulnerability is fortified by forgiveness. Forgiveness implies letting go. Letting go of the other person's energy, which you have taken on yourself. Letting go of the guilt and fear that are self-imposed. Letting go of the need to be right or to get even. Letting go, like forgiveness, truly neutralizes any current or past manipulation. ''Forgiveness doesn't mean reminding people of what they did to upset you; forgiveness doesn't mean adding instructions for future behavior. 'I forgive you, but I hope you'll be more careful' is not the model.'' (Kristen Johnson Ingram, *Blessing Your Enemies, Forgiving Your Friends.* Liguori, MO: Liguori Publications, 1993, p.60.)

Some people will go to ridiculous ends to prove they are right . . . to have the last word. Some people stay in abusive relationships, jobs, and other negative situations because they cannot let go. People can stay in these situations until they get physically ill and sometimes even die.

Life is too precious to spend it being manipulated. Yet, manipulation is rampant in our society. With the loss of predictability, with the escalation of violence fueled by fear, we see power struggles going on all around us. It is hard to remain flexible. Yet, that very openness is necessary for true communication, without which we'd be lost. What are some of the ways that we can learn to let go and not be controlled by others at the same time? We can do it by neutralizing manipulative remarks and situations, by knowing ourselves better, and by knowing our strengths and our weaknesses and being prepared to accept ourselves for who we are.

What are ways that you can let go and enjoy life more in a society that oftentimes seems out of control?

1. Every time you feel guilty, ask yourself where it comes from. Have you honestly done something that requires you to feel guilty? Have you tried to control someone else or have you hurt someone else? If so, an apology is a good beginning. If not, recognize the feeling as ghost guilt and try to find out where it comes from in your past history. The more often you do this, the more you will find yourself avoiding potential problems in current relationships, improving communication, and letting go of old hurts.

2. Every time you feel anxious or fearful, ask yourself where it comes from. If someone is threatening you with bodily harm, however, this is not the time for reminiscing. But how realistic are your fears, really? How grounded in the here and now are they? Remember the mother who worried about riding with her daughter who had a learner's permit? By recognizing where the excessive fear came from (the earlier bumper car accident), she was able to defuse some of that fear while realizing how much better things would be when the daughter got her regular license. Worrying whether or not twenty years down the road you'll end up as a bag lady living under a bridge is nonproductive. Remember our formula for fear: The more negative and unrealistic the fear, the more likely that it is an imaginary number and having an imagined impact on you.

3. Are you in a worry cycle? Almost addictively, human beings can terrorize themselves with worry. What gets your dander up? Since anger is closely linked to fear,

what gets your blood pressure rising? Reading the morning newspaper? Consider canceling it for a month and seeing what happens. Watching the evening news? Consider leaving the news turned off for a week and seeing what happens. Have politics got you steaming? Write a letter to your congressperson and express your concerns. Don't answer the phone at dinner. Get your name off the junk mail lists. Refuse to sign petitions. Or conversely, sign every petition. Learn to relax.

4. For every random act of violence you learn about, consider doing a random act of kindness. Place a flower on the doormat of a grumpy neighbor. Send a funny card to a friend. Find a local soup kitchen for the homeless and volunteer a few hours of your time.

5. Consider compromising any lifetime thinking patterns that say, "All or nothing, with no in-between." It is possible to disagree with a law, but still follow it. It is possible to disagree with another person, yet still respect that person and where he or she is coming from. It is possible that we all can win. But not by having to control one another for our own benefit. You can't win through intimidation.

6. Besides striking the word "should" from your vocabulary, consider striking the word "never." As any parent knows, saying "never" almost instantly forces you to retract the statement, as if the universe were appalled by such a negative notion. "I will *never* let my child sit in front of the television and use it like a baby-sitter." Within three days, guaranteed, just as the chain letters promise, you will be saying to the teenage neighborhood baby-sitter, "Just stick Junior here in front of the television until I get back. The dentist said my root canal won't take long."

Do you know what the real problem is with manipulation? It isn't just that you feel crummy. The problem is that manipulation destroys open communication and trust. More relationships are out of whack because of manipulation than one can begin to imagine—in friendships, in families, in the workplace, in sports, in clubs, and in groups of all kinds. You will do yourself a lifelong favor if you start today, however modestly, to stop letting yourself manipulate or be manipulated.

> ## RECOGNIZE THAT YOU ARE AN EFFECTIVE ADULT DOING THE BEST YOU CAN.

Even if you feel that you are not effective, you are. You are doing the best you can, right now, last year, and tomorrow. You are doing your best going through the process of life. And life is a process, not just a series of events. You may be able to improve on your best tomorrow, but right now you are doing the best you can. If someone tells you that you aren't, consider the source before chastising yourself. No honestlies spoken here.

To exorcise the ghosts of guilt and fear (the weapons of the manipulator), it helps to realize that the ghosts are really insubstantial. They are no longer real, if they ever were. The only reality they had was what you gave them. Guilt and fear have a basis in irrationality. When you shine the light of day (or understanding) on them, they tend to dry up and blow away. A ghost, like any other thing that goes bump in the night, exists in your bedroom when your eyes are closed. It exists in your closet and under the clothes you throw on the chair. When you open the windows and let the light stream in, it is not there anymore, because it has no substance.

So whenever you feel you are not being good enough, or whenever you feel you are not being effective enough, ask yourself, "What ghost of my past is haunting me?" *Then shine a light on it, and let it go.*

Remember how we stressed that the manipulators are actually paying you a compliment. On the one extreme, they may be envious of you, admire you, like you, and want some of your power and strength. At the other extreme, they may fear you or your behavior, which means that you still have the upper hand. And besides, there are always the bullies, whose self-esteem is so low that any target will do. Regardless of the reason, the manipulators feel compelled to try to control you. Most manipulators are not even aware that they are doing this, let alone consciously using guilt and fear as weapons.

In the authors' experience, if you use the principles and techniques, the five levels, that you've just studied here, two things usually occur. First, you are no longer a victim. And second, repeated use of these techniques in an ongoing manipulative relationship can actually change the manipulative behavior of the other person toward you for the better. The manipulator no longer can have any of your power, at best. At worst, the manipulator receives back the negative energy that he or she tried to put on you in the first place, and it doesn't feel good. Either way, you give that person ample opportunity to feel better when he or she stops manipulating you.

Sometimes, however, a manipulative relationship will not improve, even though you've tried practically everything. Sometimes the underlying forces are more complicated or the situation more severe than usual. Sometimes the relationship is an abusive one, and you need additional outside help fast. And sometimes all the self-exploration and experimentation in communication simply fail to change life for the better. Maybe you are not dealing with everyday manipulation at all. Or, maybe you've been dealt more of life's disappointments than you are statistically supposed to receive.

If you are feeling crummy and need help, *run, don't walk, to a trusted source of competent counseling.* Seek help from a psychologist or other legitimate counselor. Seek help from your minister, rabbi, or priest. Besides counseling you, these people are trained to direct you to the many outstanding support groups that exist today.

Finally, remember to let go or forgive. Forgiveness or letting go is really the first step in countering any manipulation. You are the one with the greater power and strength. With forgiving or letting go, you release and get on with your life. When you let go or forgive, you'll find a freedom from guilt and fear, a freedom that truly empowers you.

We aren't as likely to be manipulated if we know who we are and can genuinely believe in ourselves. When we know our own weaknesses and can accept them, we can forgive *ourselves.* When we can become vulnerable without fear, we can truly share ourselves with others. A large part of giving up the ghosts of the past is learning to trust ourselves. Since we can learn to trust someone else intuitively, we need to learn to trust ourselves in the same way. We need to trust our feelings. We need to communicate with those feelings. As we become more effective at communicating with others, we will learn how to communicate better with ourselves. The more we do this, the more we learn who we are.

As we learn who we are, we can ask ourselves: What do we really want from life? Quite simply, most of us want to love and to be loved in return, to nurture and to be nurtured.

As we learn who we are, we can ask ourselves: But *what* do we love?

We love that which accepts us as we are. We love knowing we are free to grow and develop and not be judged. We love the parts of us that are ours alone. We love being the child and the parent and the lover and the friend. We love peace.

Peace.